Lehman Strauss

THE ELEVEN
COMMANDMENTS

formerly "FROM SINAI TO CALVARY"

SCRIPTURE TRUTH BOOK COMPANY
Fincastle, VA

FIRST EDITION, OCTOBER 1946
As "From Sinai to Calvary"
SECOND EDITION, FEBRUARY 1955
SIXTH PRINTING, DECEMBER 1979

ISBN 0-87213-814-3
PRINTED IN THE UNITED STATES OF AMERICA

PREFACE

THE messages contained in this book were delivered to the congregation of the Calvary Baptist Church in the Spring of 1944. For five years the writer had been preaching mainly from the New Testament, emphasizing the doctrine of salvation by grace through faith. Several families, who formerly were members of the Reformed Church, made inquiry concerning the value and importance of the Mosaic Law in these days. In answer to this query, the following messages were prepared and preached. If they are used in this permanent form to bring enlightenment and blessing to those who read them, the author will be grateful to God who revealed them by His Spirit.

Acknowledgment is hereby given to the Misses Helen Hertzler and Evelyn Den Bleyker, who so ably assisted in the editing and typing of the manuscripts.

LEHMAN STRAUSS

Bristol, Pennsylvania

THE ELEVEN
COMMANDMENTS

By LEHMAN STRAUSS

CONTENTS

CONTENTS

CHAPTER I
THE SCRIPTURES AND THE LAW

CHAPTER I

THE SCRIPTURES AND THE LAW

SOME fifteen hundred years before Christ was born, Moses, under God, led the Israelites out of the bondage of the Egyptian ruler Pharaoh. They were en route to Canaan, the promised land, when they stopped to pitch camp at the foot of Mount Sinai. Here the pilgrim host was to experience a series of events and learn some never-to-be-forgotten lessons. Sinai was to be a new beginning for Israel. Up until that time, God was constantly showing forth His grace and power in behalf of His people. Blessings had been showered upon them unconditionally notwithstanding their sins and failures. But in spite of fresh displays of the lovingkindness of the Lord, Israel murmured and complained, charging God and Moses with neglect.

Thus began a new dispensation in the life of the nation Israel. Calling Moses up into the mountain, God gave him the Law. This doubtless was one of the outstanding events in human history.

Included in the Law were the Ten Commandments, sometimes called the Law of Moses. Perhaps no portion of Holy Scripture has been the object of such misunderstanding and the target of so much criticism as the Ten Commandments. Some religious leaders have made it the sole ground of man's salvation, while others have discarded it as having no value whatsoever in this age of grace. We have studied both these extreme views. Hence this introductory chapter is presented with the view to a higher concept and a true evaluation of the Mosaic Law.

A close examination of the Bible will show that all time is divided into eras, or dispensations. There are seven such periods set forth in the Scriptures. The first four of the dispensations are given little space in the Biblical records. They are fully covered in the book of Genesis and the first eighteen chapters of the book of Exodus. All that is recorded between Exodus, chapter nineteen, and Revelation, chapter twenty, has to do with the last three of the dispensations which are as follows.

1. THE DISPENSATION OF THE LAW OF MOSES

This period began with the giving of the law at Sinai, and ended with the death of Christ on the Cross at Calvary. This age is wholly past.

2. THE DISPENSATION OF GRACE

This is the present age in which we now are living. It had its commencement with the sacrifice of Christ on the cross, and it will be consummated by the return of the Lord Jesus Christ.

3. THE DISPENSATION OF THE KINGDOM

The age of the earth-reign of Christ is yet future. Its duration is for one thousand years, and it is bounded on the one hand by the Second Coming of Christ to occupy His throne in Jerusalem (Matt. 25: 31), and on the other by the ushering in of the new heavens and the new earth (Rev. 21: 1).

Dr. Lewis Sperry Chafer has said: "Due recognition of the essential character of each of these ages is the key to the understanding of the exact manner of the divine rule in each age. . . . The practice of confusing these three ages in respect to their characteristics and the manner of the Divine rule in each is common, and is, doubtless, the greatest error into which many devout Bible interpreters fall." We must bear in mind, as has been outlined above, that the age of law is sharply divided from this age of grace by the death of Jesus Christ. In keeping this truth before us we will be aided greatly to an understanding of the lawful use of the Law. The separation of the present and the preceding dispensations is shown to us by John the Baptist when he said: "The law was given by Moses, but grace and truth came by Jesus Christ" (John 1: 17).

1. THE LAW WAS ASSIGNED EXPRESSLY TO ISRAEL

The Law had its beginning at Mount Sinai, and until that time it never was revealed to, much less imposed upon, any other people. We know there was sin in the world before the Law was given, and that man died as a result of his sin, for we read: "Until the law sin was in the world. . . . Death reigned from Adam to Moses, even over them that had not sinned after the similitude of Adam's transgression" (Rom. 5: 13, 14). But at no time, from Adam to Moses, is there so much as a reference made to the laws of Sinai. When the Law was proposed, it was primarily to Israel as a nation. The few passages that follow are some of the many given to show its relation to Israel.

"Now therefore hearken, O Israel, . . . What nation is there so great, that hath statutes and judgments so righteous as all this law, which I set before you this day?" (Deut. 4: 1, 8).

"And Moses called all Israel, and said unto them, Hear, O Israel, the statutes and judgments which I speak in your ears this day, that ye may learn them, and keep, and do them" (Deut. 5: 1).

"And Jesus answered him, The first of all the commandments is, Hear, O Israel; The Lord our God is one Lord" (Mark 12: 29).

"Who are Israelites, to whom pertaineth the adoption, and the glory, and the covenants, and THE GIVING OF THE LAW" (Rom. 9: 4).

The Law of Sinai had a direct bearing upon the Jewish nation, but it has no more direct bearing upon the Christian than it had upon the human race from Adam to Moses. To the Christian it is written: "Ye are not under the law, but under grace" (Rom. 6: 14). It is said of the Gentiles that they "have not the law" (Rom. 2: 14). Surely no other words could be plainer.

2. THE LAW WAS A TEMPORARY COVENANT

God never intended that the Law should be in force permanently. The Law of Sinai was a temporary covenant given for temporary purposes. We have said that the Law as a dispensation ceased to be in force after the death of Christ. This is not man's view but rather the plain teaching of the Word of God. Four hundred and thirty years before the Law was given, God made a covenant with Abraham. He promised Abraham a "seed" through which salvation should come (Gen. 12: 3; 22: 18). The promised Seed was none other than Christ Himself—"That the blessing of Abraham might come on the Gentiles *through Jesus Christ*" (Gal. 3: 14). The Apostle adds: "Now to Abraham and his seed were the promises made. He saith not, And to seeds, as of many; but as of one, And to thy Seed, *which is Christ*" (Gal. 3: 16). The promise that God gave to Abraham was abiding and changeless. The subsequent giving of the Mosaic Law did in no way alter or affect the Abrahamic promise. It was an unconditional promise that was not fulfilled before the law was given, but instead, found its fulfilment in Christ. There was no condition of obedience to any law in the promises made to Abraham. It was a gift of grace. When the Law was given, it was added "till the Seed should come to whom the promise was made" (Gal. 3: 19). The Law was never a part of the original promise made to Abraham. It "was added," but it did not invalidate the covenant of pure grace made to Abraham.

Now that Christ has come, the Law is done away, for it is not possible for the two to co-exist. In this present age the Law is not in force, either as a basis for salvation or as the rule of the Christian's life. The salvation and the security of the soul must now be centered in the Person of Jesus Christ. He is the sole object of man's faith. Paul said: "Before faith came, we were kept under the law, shut up into the faith which should afterwards be revealed. Wherefore the law was our schoolmaster to bring us unto Christ, that we might be justified by faith. But after that faith is come, we are no longer under a schoolmaster" [the law] (Gal. 3: 23-25). Elsewhere Paul says that the law which was "written and engraven in stones . . . is done away" (2 Cor. 3: 7, 11).

The believer is one who has been "born of the Spirit" (John 3: 6) and not of the Law, "for the letter killeth, but the Spirit giveth life" (2 Cor. 3: 6). The Law is a ministration of death and condemnation while the Spirit is the ministration of life and righteousness. "The law of the Spirit of life in Christ Jesus hath made me free from the law of sin and death" (Rom. 8: 2). Christians are also led by the Spirit of God: "For as many as are led by the Spirit of God, they are the sons of God" (Rom. 8: 14). Paul concludes therefore that 'if ye be led of the Spirit, ye are not under the law" (Gal. 5: 18). Our Lord Jesus Christ "abolished in His flesh the enmity, even the law of commandments" (Eph. 2: 15). When He cried from the cross, "It is finished," He completed our salvation, "blotting out the handwriting of ordinances that was against us, which was contrary to us, and took it out of the way, nailing it to His cross" (Col. 2: 14).

3. THE LAW CANNOT BE KEPT BY MAN.

It is important that man sees himself exactly as God depicts him in His Word. Most of us flaunt our good points. We search for inherent goodness and console ourselves with the age-long saying that "There is a little bit of good in the worst of us." But listen to what God has to say.

"The imagination of man's heart is evil from his youth" (Gen. 8: 21).

"The Lord looked down from heaven upon the children of men, to see if there were any that did understand, and seek God. They are all gone aside, they are

altogether become filthy: there is none that doeth good, no not one" (Ps. 14: 2, 3).

"We are all as an unclean thing, and all our righteousnesses are as filthy rags" (Isa. 64: 6).

"The heart is deceitful above all things, and desperately wicked" (Jer. 17: 9).

"There is not a just man upon earth, that doeth good, and sinneth not" (Eccl. 7: 20).

"There is none that understandeth, there is none that seeketh after God" (Rom. 3: 11).

"There is none that doeth good, no, not one" (Rom. 3: 12).

"For all have sinned, and come short of the glory of God" (Rom. 3: 23).

"If we say that we have no sin, we deceive ourselves, and the truth is not in us" (1 John 1: 8).

Thus we have God's view of the heart of man. Now we know that the Lord is holy and that He hates sin. Furthermore, His holiness and righteous judgments demand that sin be punished. How to escape the condemnation of Almighty God is the big issue that confronts the sinner. We know that "whatsoever a man soweth, that shall he also reap" (Gal. 6: 7), therefore the heart cries with one of old: "How then can man be justified with God?" (Job 25: 4). Certainly it is not by the keeping of the Law, for not one of us can fully or satisfactorily keep it.

The Apostle Paul wrote: "The carnal mind is enmity against God: for *it is not subject to the law of God*, neither indeed can be" (Rom. 8: 7). Even if man would desire to subject himself to the law of God, he would find himself helpless to do so. The flesh, the hideously corrupt state of man, renders the law helpless. The Law can forbid, rebuke, and curse sin, but it cannot take it away. When we would do good we find that evil is present with us. The flesh "is not subject to the law of God." Since God gave the tables of stone to Moses there has been universal failure in keeping the law. Because of the universal failure to observe the law, it became a curse. This is difficult teaching for many to receive because they feel that if one does the best he can, that will be enough. But the Scripture says: "As many as are of the works of the law are under the curse: for it is written, Cursed is every one that continueth not in *all things* which are written in the book of the law to do them" (Gal. 3: 10). The Apostle Paul quoted this verse from Deut. 27: 26, and it means simply that the Law never offered a reward for keeping some part of it, but that it always imposed a penalty for breaking any part of it. The Law demanded absolute perfection; it never required anyone to do the best he could. "For I testify again to every man that is circumcised, that he is a debtor to do the *whole law*" (Gal. 5: 3). The Apostle James adds: "For whosoever shall keep the whole law, and yet offend in one point, *he is guilty of all*" (James 2: 10).

4. THE LAW IS POWERLESS TO SAVE

"For what the law *could not do*, in that *it was weak* through the flesh, God sending His own Son in the likeness of sinful flesh, and for sin condemned sin in the flesh" (Rom. 8: 3). God never purposed that the Law should make a man righteous. That was something "the Law could not do, in that it was weak." The sinner's redemption was planned by God in eternity past. Jesus was the Lamb slain before the foundation of the world. By His death Christ has redeemed us from eternal death and condemnation, the penalty of a broken law. "Christ hath redeemed us from the curse of the law, being made a curse for us: for it is written, Cursed is every one that hangeth on a tree" (Gal. 3: 13). Though the Law was given to reveal righteousness, it never was intended to create righteousness. It could not. "Christ is the end of the law for righteousness to every one that believeth" (Rom. 10: 4).

The Law is holy, just, and good; but it is the symbol of bondage. When I was a boy I attended a Sunday School where it was required of me to memorize the Ten Commandments. I knew them by heart and could repeat them with accuracy whenever I was called upon. I was in three different departments of the Sunday School and sat under six different teachers. Each teacher began with her new scholar by making sure he or she knew the Ten Commandments. After several years of studying the law, I was still a poor helpless sinner on my way to Hell. Then one day I was introduced to the grace of God in Christ. I saw my sins and Jesus hanging on Calvary's cross for me. I cried to God for mercy, and discovered by experience that, what the Law could not do, Jesus already had done for me—"For by grace are ye saved through faith."

"Free from the Law! O happy condition!
Jesus has bled, and there is remission."

5. THE LAWFUL USE OF THE LAW

"Wherefore then serveth the law?" (Gal. 3: 19). Having seen from the Scriptures that man cannot keep the Law, and that the Law itself is powerless to save, Paul asks the question: "Wherefore then serveth the law?" If it will not save anyone, what use is there for it? If it does not answer the need of man's soul, is it not useless altogether? Since our salvation is complete in Jesus Christ, and the Law does not serve as a means of salvation, what practical good can I derive from the Law? These and many other questions enter the minds of those who hear for the first time that the Law contributes nothing toward taking a man to Heaven.

The Law is not something to be despised, "but we know that the law is good, if a man use it lawfully" (1 Tim. 1: 8). If we use the Law for the purpose for which God gave it, we will profit thereby. It is lawful to use the Law as a means to an end, but it is unlawful to make it an end in itself. What, then, is the lawful use of the Law?

Paul said to Timothy: "The law is not made for a righteous man, but for the lawless and disobedient, for the ungodly and for sinners" (1 Tim. 1: 9). We see here that the Law has no application to a righteous person. The Christian, having been saved by grace, is dead to the Law. But the Law was given to reveal sin and to make sin appear exceeding sinful. This was the personal testimony of the Apostle Paul when he said: "I had not known sin, but by the law: for I had not known lust, except the law had said, Thou shalt not covet" (Rom. 7: 7). Where there is no law there is no consciousness of sin. Without a mirror, I may not discover that my face is dirty. God uses the Law as a mirror, for "what things soever the law saith, it saith to them who are under the law: that every mouth may be stopped, and all the world may become guilty before God" (Rom. 3: 19). In revealing sin, the Law has efficiently done its work. It cannot function beyond that point, for "by the deeds of the law there shall no flesh be justified in His sight: for by the law is the *knowledge of sin*" (Rom. 3: 20). In order to have your sin removed you must come to the Lord Jesus Christ because "the blood of Jesus Christ His Son cleanseth us from all sin" (1 John 1: 7).

The beacon light can show the way to port, but it cannot loose the storm-driven ship from the rocks. The Law points us to the holy Mount, but it can never bring us to the top.

"Run and work! the law commands,
But gives me neither feet nor hands;
But sweeter sounds the gospel brings:
It bids me fly, and gives me wings."

Salvation from sin is by the grace of God and not by the Law of Moses. "For by grace are ye saved through faith; and that not of yourselves: it is the gift of God: not of works, lest any man should boast" (Eph. 2: 8, 9). If the Law, which was given fifteen hundred years before Christ came, could have saved man and taken him to Heaven, then God erred greatly in permitting His only begotten Son to die the awful death by crucifixion. But, thank God, it is "not by works of righteousness which we have done, but according to His mercy He saved us, by the washing of regeneration, and renewing of the Holy Ghost" (Titus 3: 5). No, dear reader, God made no mistake

when He sent Jesus Christ to the cross, "for if right-
ousness came by the law, then Christ is dead in vain"
(Gal. 2: 21).

>*"Free from the law! O happy condition!*
>*Jesus hath bled, and there is remission:*
>*Cursed by the law and bruised by the fall,*
>*Christ hath redeemed us, once for all."*

Must we conclude, therefore, that the Law has ceased
to be of any value whatever to the Christian? The
Christian did not receive life by the Law, nor is the
Law the rule of life after a man has been saved. Christ
is our life and our rule of life. "For in Christ Jesus
neither circumcision availeth anything, nor uncircum-
cision, but a new creature (or *new creation*). And as
many walk according to *this rule* (the *new creation*),
peace be on them, and mercy, and upon the Israel of
God" (Gal. 6: 15, 16). In answering the question asked
at the beginning of this paragraph, we only say that
Exodus, chapter twenty, is as much a part of the Canon
of Scripture as is any other chapter in the Bible. Inasmuch as *"All Scripture* is given by inspiration of God,
and is profitable for doctrine, for reproof, for correc-
tion, for instruction in righteousness: that the man of
God may be perfect, thoroughly furnished unto all
good works" (2 Tim. 3: 16, 17), I invite you to share
with me in these sermons just as we would consider
any other text in the Word of God.

THE SOVEREIGNTY OF GOD

THE FIRST COMMANDMENT

"Thou shalt have no other gods before Me"
(Exod. 20: 3).

CHAPTER II

THE SOVEREIGNTY OF GOD

"Thou shalt have no other gods before Me"
(Exodus 20: 3).

THE Law reaches in two directions, Godward and manward. The first four commandments show us man's responsibility toward God, and the last six commandments deal with man's relationship to his fellowman. This is the divinely arranged order. It is necessary that we be brought face to face with God first, for unless we have in our minds and hearts the proper conception of God and our responsibilities toward Him, we shall fail in our associations with the rest of the world.

1. THE CLAIM

The subject matter of this present chapter is *God*. It is but appropriate that we begin with Him. The first commandment is prefaced by a brief declarative statement—"I am the Lord thy God. . . . Thou shalt have no other gods before Me." It begins by boldly asserting the reality of God. It assumes that God is. The ancient philosophers endeavored to think through the mystery of godliness. They tried to prove or disprove the existence of God. But the first commandment is in harmony with all the rest of the Word of

God. None of the writers questions the existence of God. They delight in Him. They assume His existence and acknowledge His sovereignty. Though there is sufficient evidence to prove that God is, He is beyond finite reasoning and human analysis. It is asked in the book of Job: "Canst thou by searching find out God?" (Job 11: 7). The man of wisdom replies: "No man can find out the work that God maketh from the beginning to the end" (Eccl. 3: 11). The Apostle Paul cried: "How unsearchable are His judgments, and His ways past finding out!" (Rom. 11: 33).

When God said: "I am the Lord thy God," we know that He was addressing Israel. But the application is universal and eternal. God declares His eternality and self-existence in the divine name, "*I am Jehovah*." No mortal has fathomed the deep significance of this name by which God declares Himself. Dr. G. Campbell Morgan has pointed out that the name JEHOVAH is a combination of three Hebrew words that mean "He that will be, He that is, He that was." If, by any stretch of the imagination, we were to look back into eternity past, we would hear God say: "I am He that was." If we concentrate on the present moment with all its recent discoveries and progress, we hear God say: "I am He that is." And if we peer into eternity future, we hear God say: "I am He that will be." Puny man errs greatly when he reckons in any age without God.

A significant passage will serve well here. While Moses was still keeping the flocks of Jethro, his father-in-law, God appeared to him on the backside of the desert. Suddenly there appeared to Moses a burning bush that was not consumed. Out of the fire came the voice of God saying: "Come now therefore, and I will send thee unto Pharaoh, that thou mayest bring forth My people the children of Israel out of Egypt" (Exod. 3: 10). Feeling his own insufficiency for the work, Moses offered God four excuses why he should not be the man for the task. Finally, God gave Moses the authority by which he should speak to the people —"Thus shalt thou say unto the children of Israel, I AM hath sent me unto you" (Exod. 3: 14). Here we have God revealing Himself for the first time as the self-existent, eternal, ever-acting One.

Upon this statement rests the authority of God. He is before all things, and by Him all things consist. God is sovereign, and upon the fact of His supremacy, His authority over all things, He issues His commands to His creature. The first words in the Bible are: "In the beginning God. . . . " These words place the Almighty in the attitude of primacy and power. We must begin with God for He is sovereign over all. When God sent fire and brimstone upon Sodom and Gomorrah and held back the waters of the Red Sea, He showed that He was sovereign over the realm of nature. By casting Satan out of Heaven and by over-powering the demons in men, God displayed sovereignty over the realm of spirits. He created man from the dust of the earth, pronounced the death-sentence upon him when Adam sinned, and struck dead Nadab and Abihu and others. Thereby He demonstrates His sovereignty over men's bodies. God only can forgive sins and reconcile man unto Himself. This He does, and thus shows that He is sovereign over men's souls.

We need a God like this. The marvel is that men shut Him out of their lives and live as though there were no God. Recently a group of girls who were leaving a factory on Friday night after completing their week's work, found it was raining rather hard, and several of the group began to curse and damn the weather. This is practical atheism and is typical of a universal condition. We fail to realize that the times and the seasons God keeps in His own power. The scientists tell us there are laws of nature, but we know that behind all of nature there is God. How thankful we should be that He makes the rain to fall and the sun to shine on the just and the unjust. Too often, by wishful thinking and occupation with our own selves and our egotistical interests, we fail to give God His rightful place.

2. THE COMMANDMENT

"Thou shalt have no other gods before Me." Since God is what He claims to be, then He must be the one Object of worship. Since God creates and sustains man, it is reasonable that He should make such a claim upon His creature. The commandment allows for no compromise. Israel was to worship no other gods as a substitute for Jehovah, nor to worship other gods in addition to the worship of Jehovah.

After studying the non-Christian religions of the world, we are convinced that enthroned in every man's heart is a god whom he worships. Doubtless the god at the centre of many lives is a false god. Nevertheless, there is something which every man worships. Someone has said that when man dethrones God, he deifies and worships himself. Luther said: "That upon which you set your heart and put your trust is properly your God." We have seen that God has laid claim to being

the only one eternal and perfect God. Upon the veracity
of that claim He commands: "Thou shalt have no
other gods before Me."

The commandment is one against idolatry. Since
man must have a god and has not the true God, he
invents a god to suit himself. This is a common practice among civilized people as well as among uncivilized. It was sadly true in Israel only a short time
after the Decalouge had been given. Moses had returned to the top of the Mount to receive further
instructions from the Lord. "And when the people
saw that Moses delayed to come down out of the
mount, the people gathered themselves together unto
Aaron, and said unto him, Up, make us gods, which
shall go before us" (Exod. 32: 1). How tragic! "*Make
us gods!*" They became weary of waiting upon God
whom they could not see with the eye and created for
themselves a visible counterfeit. Aaron, submitting to
the demand of the people, asked for their golden ear-
rings, and made them into a molten calf, fashioning it
with a graving tool. The people bowed themselves
before it, and cried: "These be thy gods, O Israel,
which brought thee up out of the land of Egypt"
(Exod. 32: 4). This is typical of the human heart.
It seeks after that which can be seen and which satis-
fies the senses. The Church has suffered because men
have turned from the unseen realities of Heaven to
the visible earthly imitations. With "graving tool" in
hand, some of the church-leaders have made false gods,
and the people bow down to them.

The Bible contains accurate accounts of men bowing
before false gods. Think of *Baal-peor*, the god of the
Moabites, who was worshipped in services openly im-

pure and licentious (Num. 25: 1-3); *Baal-zebub,* the
lord of the fly, who was worshipped at Ekron (2 Kings
1: 2, 3); *Moloch,* the fire-god of the children of Ammon,
who was worshipped in acts of most awful and degraded cruelty; and that of *Mammon* which "debased
its devotees to the lust which dreams that power lurks
in possession." It all sounds so heathenish and uncivilized that we are undone when we realize that there
is a duplication of just such gross idolatry in the
civilized nations of the world in the twentieth century.

The commandment forbidding idolatry had no sooner
been given than it was broken. And for nearly thirty-
five hundred years since the Law was issued, man has
denied the one true and living God, set up his false
gods, and ignorantly worshipped them. Some of these
idols have been the sun, moon, stars, images, statues,
pictures, trees, and animals. Since man's understanding has been darkened by sin, he has not had the
right conception of God. But when Jesus Christ came
into the world, He revealed God to man. The mission
of Christ was to lead the Father into full view. "No
man hath seen God at any time; the only begotten
Son, which is in the bosom of the Father, He hath
declared Him" [or made Him known] (John 1: 18).
Now all who are in Christ have viewed the Father.
Jesus said: "He that hath seen Me hath seen the
Father" (John 14: 9). "I and the Father are one"
(John 10: 30 R.V.).

3. THE CHRISTIAN

The moment a person becomes a Christian he enters
into a new relationship. Unbelievers are without Christ,
without hope and without God (Eph. 2: 12). Chris-

tians are called sons of God by faith in Christ Jesus (Gal. 3: 26). Upon entering this new life the believer is faced with the eternal truth of the first commandment, that God is sovereign and that He demands first place in the heart and the affections of His children. We have stated that men in Old Testament times had false gods because they failed to conceive the nature of the true God. It is not until the Christian becomes intimately acquainted with Jehovah—Jesus in the New Testament that he ceases to have any other gods. Let there be no mistake in our minds concerning the Deity of Jesus Christ. The "I AM" of the burning bush and of the first commandment is none other than Jesus Christ of the New Testament. Christ is the express Image of God's Person and the effulgence of His glory. Jesus is God. All of the attributes of Deity are ascribed to Him. He is holy (John 6: 69), *eternal* (John 17: 5), *immutable* (Heb. 13: 8), *omnipotent* (Matt. 28: 18), *omniscient* (John 16: 30), *omnipresent* (Matt. 18: 20; 28: 20). As we see who Jesus is, the New Testament enforcement of the Law begins to lay hold upon us.

When writing to Christians, the Apostle John said: "Little children, keep yourselves from idols" (1 John 5: 21). The command to abstain from idolatry is needed no less today than it was in Moses' day. It grieved the Apostle Paul while in Athens "when he saw the city wholly given to idolatry" (Acts 17: 16). Elsewhere Paul says that idolatry is one of the "works of the flesh" (Gal. 5: 19, 20). Christians are exhorted to "mortify therefore your members which are upon the earth; fornication, uncleanness, inordinate affection,

evil concupiscence, and covetousness, which is idolatry"
(Col. 3:5). My contention is that God, in this age
of grace, has not given up His claim to sovereignty
nor has He made void the command that men should
worship Him and have no other god. Jesus said:
"Thou shalt worship the Lord thy God, and Him only
shalt thou serve" (Matt. 4:10). Again He said:
"Thou shalt love the Lord thy God with all thy heart,
and with all they soul, and with all thy mind. This is
the first and great commandment" (Matt. 22:37, 38).

ARE CHRISTIANS GUILTY OF IDOLATRY?

Not only was the Jew guilty of idolatry, but the
modern Christian also can be charged with the violation of the law that forbids this. I am well aware
of the fact that some of you will protest the application of this commandment to the Christian. However,
all I ask is that you share with me in the New Testament passages that follow.

Some Christians worship *the god of money.* The
Apostle Paul expressly declared this to be idol-worship
when he spoke of "covetousness, which is idolatry"
(Col. 3:5). We agree that the Israelites practised
idolatry when they worshipped the golden calf, yet we
Americans are equally as guilty in our worship of the
"golden eagle." Our American money bears the inscription, "In God we trust." Someone has suggested
that we alter it to read: "In *this* god we trust." The
ancient patriarch Job has said: "If I have made gold
my hope, or have said to the fine gold, Thou art my
confidence; if I rejoiced because my wealth was great,
and because mine hand had gotten much . . . I should
have denied the God that is above" (Job 31:24, 25, 28).

This is exactly what our Lord meant when He said: "Ye cannot serve God and mammon" (Matt. 6:24). Paul said: "a covetous man who is an idolater" (Eph. 5:5).

A story in one of McGuffey's readers tells of a miser who had under his basement a secret sub-basement known to no one but himself. Here he hoarded large sums of silver and gold. Daily he would come in secrecy to worship. He delighted to run his bony fingers through the coins and listen to the music of their clank, as he said: "O my Beauties, O my Beauties!" One day while he sat worshipping the god of gold, a breeze blew the door of the sub-basement shut. A spring lock that could be turned only from the outside fastened the door. The miser was shut in with his gold and his god. Years later when the old house was being torn down, some men came across his skeleton stretched over the pile of gold and silver. He made money his god, and the god had finally destroyed him.

Now money is not to be disdained. Frugality is not to be frowned upon. There is no virtue in being a pauper. Money honestly earned and wisely used can bring untold blessing. Someone has said: "I can take a dollar and use it so that the eagle upon it will turn vulture and tear at somebody's heart. But I can also take that same dollar and so use it that the eagle upon it will become a mocking-bird to make music in somebody's soul." Not one of us would sanction the worship of Baal or Moloch, yet we put Mammon into the first place in our lives. "The Mammon of unrighteousness" is the god before whom some Christians bow daily. "The love of money is the root of all evil;"

and if this disease is not checked, it will eat like a canker.

Next comes *the god of pleasure*. Paul spoke of those who are "lovers of pleasure more than lovers of God" (2 Tim. 3:4). Mark me! I am not despising pleasure and pastime. "All work and no play makes Jack a dull boy." But all play and no work makes Jack an idolater. The one purpose some folk seem to have in life is to find excitement and to have a good time. Pleasure is not sinful in itself provided it is not sinful pleasure. The body demands recreation and diversion, the kind that strengthens one physically, mentally, and morally. But to become a slave to pleasure makes one a dissipated idolater. Riches and pleasure become idols of this world when they are permitted to engross us.

Another idol is *the god of the belly*. Does the suggestion seem vulgar to you? Yet Paul by the Holy Spirit speaks of those "whose god is their belly" (Phil. 3:19). There are those who are engrossed in self-indulgence, slaves to the sensual appetites, and "they that are such serve not our Lord Jesus Christ, but their own belly" (Rom. 16:18). The table has become their altar, and their motto is: "Let us eat, drink, and be merry, for tomorrow we die." I am reminded of a certain man whose wife is deprived of worship in the house of God every Sunday morning simply because he insists upon having his dinner promptly at twelve o'clock. Like the gods of gold and pleasure, the god of sensual appetite will destroy us unless we turn from it and give Jesus Christ first place in our lives.

Then there are Christians who worship *the god of fashion*. It has been said, "Cleanliness is next to godliness." Our bodies and our clothing should be kept neat and clean, but the adornment of the body has become the idol of many. The Bible says: "In like manner also, that women adorn themselves in modest apparel, with shamefacedness and sobriety; not with broided hair, or gold, or pearls, or costly array; but (which becometh women professing godliness) with good works" (1 Tim. 2: 9, 10). Some Christians own they stay away from church because their clothing is "not good enough." The adorning of the true child of God is not the "outward adorning. . . . but let it be the hidden man of the heart, in that which is not corruptible, even the ornament of a meek and quiet spirit, which is in sight of God of great price" (1 Pet. 3: 3, 4). When Christ occupies the throne of the heart, the god of fashion will have been cast out.

Finally, there are those who make an idol out of *the Holy Bible.* Too many people have little more than a superstitious regard for the Word of God. They look upon it as being somewhat of a lucky charm. An expensively-bound Bible is purchased only to be left lying in some place where it can be looked upon but never read, much less studied. It is the common practice that a copy of the New Testament or a Bible be carried on the person of many of our service-men going overseas to battle. Often this Book is not studied nor practised, but serves, in the minds of the bearers, as some sort of charm for protection. This is akin to the wearing of Roman medals and the carrying of prayer-books for the same purpose. If your Bible serves for nothing more than a household god, then you are guilty of idolatry.

We have mentioned but five of the present-day gods of professing Christians, but they will serve to show us that the sin of idolatry prevails in our midst. There is spiritual truth to be learned and applied from the first commandment. Let us get alone with our God and Saviour Jesus Christ, the God who was, who is, and who will be; and if we can discover any one thing or any one person in the life that relegates God into the background, we must confess the sin of idolatry, cast out the idol, and bow down to the Lordship of Jesus Christ.

THE STANDARD FOR WORSHIP

THE SECOND COMMANDMENT

"Thou shalt not make unto thee any graven image, or any likeness of any thing that is in heaven above, or that is in the earth beneath, or that is in the water under the earth. Thou shalt not bow down thyself to them, nor serve them: for I the Lord thy God am a jealous God, visiting the iniquity of the fathers upon the children unto the third and fourth generation of them that hate Me; and showing mercy unto thousands of them that love Me, and keep My commandments"

(Exod. 20: 4-6).

THE STANDARD FOR WORSHIP

"Thou shalt not make unto thee any graven image, or any likeness of anything that is in heaven above, or that is in the earth beneath, or that is in the water under the earth. Thou shalt not bow down thyself to them, nor serve them: for I the Lord thy God am a jealous God, visiting the iniquity of the fathers upon the children unto the third and fourth generation of them that hate Me; and showing mercy unto thousands of them that love Me, and keep My commandments" (Exod. 20: 4-6).

THE first and second commandments are closely related; yet there is a distinction between them that must be clearly noted. The two are not to be united, though I believe that both the Lutheran and the Roman Catholic Churches consider them one commandment. The first commandment tells us *whom* we must worship, while the second tells us *how* we must worship Him. The teaching of the first commandment is that there is only one true God to be worshipped. The teaching of the second is that God is a Spirit, and therefore He can be worshipped in spirit and in truth only. The first forbids false gods. The second forbids false worship of the true God.

There never has been a race of people, civilized or uncivilized, that has not had a god whom that race worshipped. Not one person was ever born an atheist.

Dr. Boardman has said that if a man becomes an atheist it is because "he has suicidally emasculated his own moral nature." Every child of Adam has an innate sense of God. Both Adam and Eve were in very close communion with God before the fall. Their first offspring, Cain and Abel, worshipped God with their offerings. God-consciousness is something that was handed down to us from the garden of Eden. Wherever travelers have gone—in the interior of the dark continent, in the jungles, in the polar regions, or to the islands of the sea—there never has been found a race or a tribe that did not worship some sort of god. A man may have been educated to believe that there is no God, but every man has some kind of god of his own. Man, therefore, worships almost as instinctively as he breathes. But perverted ideas regarding God have guided man's effort to worship in the wrong direction. The correct standard for worship demands a correct knowledge of the One who is to be worshipped.

1. THE CONCEPTION OF GOD.

Man's worship of God is not correct until he has the right concept of God. When Jesus spoke to the woman at the well He said: "*God is a Spirit*: and they that worship Him must worship Him in spirit and in truth" (John 4: 24). The Samaritan woman did not know the true nature of God. She looked upon the Almighty as one would look upon a mere earthly monarch, and if one would approach Him, she thought it would have to be at some designated place. Hence her statement: "Our fathers worshipped in this mountain; and ye say, that in Jerusalem is the place where men ought to worship" (ver. 20). It is evident that this poor deluded woman did not know that the infinite God was a life-giving Spirit. Her statement brought forth from our Lord the charge: "Ye worship ye know not what" (ver. 22). Like her, too many people are under the false impression that the true approach to God is by way of Mount Gerizim, Mount Zion, or some other mount. Some feel that if they are not at Jerusalem with all of the available rites, ritual, and ceremony, they cannot worship God. Like the woman of Sychar, they limit God to their own finite conceptions of Him; and while they argue to defend their pet denomination and its standard for worship, they are without God and without hope in this world.

Jesus taught this social outcast at Samaria a lesson that all men must learn. He dismissed both Gerizim and Jerusalem as essential places to worship God. He showed that the standard for worship was not made by man, and that an approach to God was not mental or physical, but spiritual. He revealed the fact that there was nothing in this world that could serve as an approach to God. Since the nature of the Almighty is not material, no material representative can be used as a platform for the worship of the Eternal One. Any idolatrous representation of Deity shows that man neither knows nor understands God.

It was the false concept of God that caused men to seek an approach through idols and images. When any man makes a false representation of God, he must beware, for it is an easy matter to slip into the act of worshipping the representation itself. Paul said they thus "changed . . . the uncorruptible God into an image made like to corruptible man, and to birds, and four-footed beasts, and creeping things" (Rom. 1:23).

Since God is a Spirit, the natural or unregenerate man, not having been born of the Spirit, cannot worship God. Worshipping in spirit and in truth is a matter of the heart, and it is possible only with true believers in the Lord Jesus Christ who possesses the Holy Spirit, for He alone can make such worship possible. The Apostle Paul wrote: "For we are the circumcision, which worship God in the spirit, and rejoice in Christ Jesus, and have no confidence in the flesh" (Phil. 3:3).

We need only to turn to Jesus Christ of Nazareth to have a perfect conception of God. He declared: "I and the Father are one" (John 10:30). "He that hath seen Me hath seen the Father" (John 14:9). Matthew, citing the prophetic Scripture, said: "Behold, a virgin shall be with child, and shall bring forth a Son, and they shall call His name Emmanuel, which being interpreted is, *God with us*" (Matt. 1:23). John the Baptist states that it is Christ's office to make God known—"No man hath seen God at any time; the only begotten Son, which is in the bosom of the Father, He hath declared Him" (John 1:18). Christ's voice is the voice of the Father—"God, who at sundry times and in divers manners spake in time past unto the fathers by the prophets, hath in these last days spoken unto us by (or in) His Son" (Heb. 1:1,2). The Apostle Paul said that we have been given "the light of the knowledge of the glory of God in the face of Jesus Christ" (2 Cor. 4:6). Writing to the Colossians he set forth Jesus as "the image of the invisible God" (1:15), and then he declared that "in Him dwelleth all the fulness of the Godhead bodily" (2:9). When we have acknowledged the Saviourhood and Lordship of Christ, we have seen God, and we need no false representation to aid us in worshipping Him.

The natural man has not the Spirit of God. He is "dead in trespasses and sins" (Eph. 2: 1). Until he is born again by the Spirit he has no spiritual consciousness, and since it is the spiritual sense in man that recognizes God, the man who has been quickened or made alive in Christ is the only one who can commune directly with God. We do not doubt for one moment that the unsaved man would like to worship God, but we insist that he is not able. Evidently man knew he was getting nowhere in his effort to worship God, so he began to make images and pictures to aid him in his worship. This is exactly what is forbidden by God in the second commandment.

2. THE COMMANDMENT OF GOD.

God had said: "Thou shalt not make unto thee any graven image, or any likeness of any thing that is in heaven above, or that is in the earth beneath, or that is in the water under the earth. Thou shalt not bow down thyself to them, nor serve them."

Invariably the question arises as to whether or not the second commandment forbids the use of every form of art as idolatrous. This would include drawings, pictures, engravings, sculpture, and many other kinds of æsthetic art. There are some Christians who refuse to have their photographs taken and who would not allow the photograph of another person in their houses.

Such is not the interpretation of this commandment. If this were God's intention, then He violated His own command shortly after He issued it to Moses, for there was no finer and more exquisite display of art than that which we find in the Tabernacle and Priesthood of Israel. The coverings, curtains, and hangings were rare works of art. In the very holy of holies there were two cherubim, covering the Mercy-Seat with their wings, one at one end and one at the other end of the Mercy-Seat. The garments of the priest consisted of an embroidered linen coat; a girdle of fine twined linen, and blue, and purple, and scarlet, of needlework, *as the Lord commanded Moses* (Exod. 39: 29). The robe of the ephod was a woven work of art, and fastened upon the hem were golden bells and pomegranates. Truly God had a conception of art and an originality that surpassed anything that man could conceive. We cannot help but feel that the Lord taught the blending of materials and colors and the engraving of wood, stone, and precious metals for man to develop and to enjoy. No; the second commandment does not forbid the use of art in worship.

What God does forbid in the second commandment is any attempt on the part of man to represent God by any natural means. This is prohibited simply because God is a Spirit and He must be worshipped in spirit and in truth. When Paul came to Athens he stood in the Areopagus, that is, in the midst of the council. He later wrote: "As I passed by, and beheld your devotions, I found an altar with this inscription, TO THE UNKNOWN GOD" (Acts 17: 23). The Athenians knew that there was a God, but their problem was the problem of all paganism and of every unregenerate person. He existed, but to them He was not known personally. They had never come into His own blessed presence. Therefore they resorted to means devised by their own hands in an endeavor to approach Him. In his commentary on the Book of the Acts, Dr. Morgan describes the scene thus: "There at his feet as he stood on that stone of impudence, was the Theseum, the wonderful Doric temple, which abides even unto this hour, one of the most perfect examples of art. On his right stretched the upper city, the Acropolis; and there, in all its significance, the Parthenon devoted to the worship of Athene. Everywhere were altars and temples and images; statuary the most beautiful and perfect, in marble, in stone, in gold, in silver, in bronze, and in wood."

The temples and the idols proved that the people were very religious, and showed a sincerity in their desire to worship. But these poor deluded dupes of Satan were trying to worship a God they never knew. Hence they surrounded themselves with representations of Deity. In His masterful address before them, the Apostle said: "Forasmuch then as we are the offspring of God, we ought not to think that the Godhead is like unto gold or silver, or stone, graven by art and man's device" (Acts 17: 29). Knowing that Paul was thoroughly trained in the Mosaic Law, we believe that he evidently had the second commandment in mind, for he declared to them, "God that made the world and all things therein, seeing that He is Lord of heaven and earth, dwelleth not in temples made with hands" (Acts 17: 24).

Since the Mosaic Law was given there never has been an age that could not be charged with violating the second commandment. Right down to our own day idols and images play an important part of the worship-service, particularly in the Roman Catholic Church. Great idol processions were common in the days before the Reformation. In some countries that are predominantly Catholic, they are still held. In Popish lands where people are kept in the dark as to the plain teaching of the Word of God, such pageants are conducted today. Such processions, even if they be "Penitential Processions," are purely pagan, and have not the approval of God upon them. How foolish of anyone to "expect any good from gods that cannot move from one place to another, unless they are carried." The Prophet Isaiah said: "They lavish gold out of the bag, and weigh silver in the balance, and hire a goldsmith; and he maketh it a god: they fall down, yea, they worship" (46:6). "They that make a graven image are all of them vanity" (44:9).

We are told that in Mexico the vain practice of bowing down to idols is carried out. At certain periods, the images of gods are carried out of the city in a mourning procession, as if they were taking their leave of it; and then, after a time, they are brought back to it again with demonstrations of joy. The Catholic Church has been guilty of this as well as of other forms of idolatry such as the worship of the relics of the saints and the bones of martyrs. During the writing of this book, the following announcement received front page recognition in a local paper. "Pilgrims from New York, New Jersey, and Pennsylvania are expected to visit the Shrine of the True Cross, to honor the relic of the true cross." The Rev. Alexander Hislop in "The Two Babylons" writes of the Church of Rome clothing and crowning images with lavish garments and diadems, as though they were ordinary mortals of living flesh and blood, worshipping the sacred heart, known as the "Rosary of the Sacred Heart," using burning lamps and wax candles, and making the sign of the cross.

The Church has been blessed with mighty men like John Knox and "sturdy Oliver Cromwell, who, as he marched here and there through Britain, mutilated with sabre and gun the statue of this or that saint in the English Cathedrals." Cromwell saw that when a man got a false idea of God through images and systems of worship, he was apt to become as false as his imaginary god. Images, idols, and pictures but tend to obliterate from our vision the true God. Any and every attempt to worship God through images and idols hides God Himself from our vision.

We have spoken of the Roman Catholic Church and its worship of images, but alas, we of the Protestant Church are guilty of bowing down before our creeds, ceremonies, candles, and crosses! Some churches feel that these things are conducive to worship. But where have we learned our ecclesiasticism? Certainly not from the first Christian Church at Jerusalem! If all this ritual and ceremony were needed to approach God, surely the Holy Spirit would have guided the Apostles in recording it in the New Testament. But we know that it was a papal practice handed down through the centuries and adopted by many of the Protestant denominations. Someone once asked, "If I have a picture of Christ in my heart, why not one upon canvas?" Another has answered, "Because the picture in the heart is capable of change and improvement, as we ourselves change and improve; the picture on canvas is fixed, and holds us to old conceptions which we should outgrow." Indeed, our Lord guarded against anyone making an image of Himself. He left no pictures, portraits, or sculptured likenesses of Himself, for He was God, and against such there is a law. All that the world has had of Jesus Christ, from a human likeness, have been artists' conceptions. You gullible Christians who have been carried away to tears and sacrificial giving by the artistic work of man will someday make the discovery that your Saviour never looked like the image on the canvas.

3. THE CHRISTIAN AND GOD

Christ is the only perfect visible Image of the one perfect invisible God and therefore can be the only Object of worship by one who has been redeemed into God's family. When God said: "Thou shalt not make unto thee any graven image," He referred to any likeness of human construction. However, here is the Divine Image before whom all of God's children must bow, the Lord Jesus Christ, "Who is the Image of the Invisible God" (Col. 1: 15). This same Jesus, not of human origin, but conceived by the Holy Ghost, is the Brightness of God's glory, and the express Image of His Person (Heb. 1: 3). How presumptuous and foolish man is when he undertakes to make another!

There is clear and definite Bible teaching relative to the image of God in all those who have been redeemed by the power of the blood of Christ. When God created man, He stamped the Divine Image on His creature. "God said, Let Us make man in Our image . . . so God created man in His own *image*" (Gen. 1: 26, 27). Adam bore the image of God in paradise, being endowed with perfect knowledge, righteousness, and holiness. When Adam fell he no longer could mirror God. He lost the God-likeness with which he was created.

But, oh, the condescending grace and mercy of God! To think that the Divine Image is yet to be restored in the children of God is beyond human comprehension! God's marked-out destiny for His own is to conform them to the image of His Son, "For whom He did foreknow, He also did predestinate to be conformed to the image of His Son" (Rom. 8: 29). Think of it! Conformed to *His* image, lacking nothing. Conformed to His image—in holiness, humility, grace, and glory.

While we wait for His coming and the transfiguration of our lives to His own, our Heavenly Father desires that our hearts be so taken up with the Lord Jesus that other people will see His likeness in us now. "But we all, with open (or unveiled) face, beholding as in a glass the glory of the Lord, are changed into the same image from glory to glory, even as by the Spirit of the Lord" (2 Cor. 3: 18).

The story is told of a lad who lived in a village at the foot of a mountain. On the profile of that mountain had been formed the image of "The Great Stone Face," looking benignly and steadfastly down upon the people. There was a legend that one day there would come to that village a person who would resemble in every detail "the great stone face." When he would come he would perform wonderful deeds and bring great blessing to the people of the village. The legend gripped a young lad who lived in the village, and often he would hide himself away, look for hours at a time at the great stone face, and think of and hope for the one who would someday come. Years passed, and still the promised one did not come; but the lad who now had become a young man, continued to spend much time admiring and reflecting upon the beauty of the great stone face. More years passed, and the young man passed from youth to middle age; still he believed the legend. Finally, when old age had overtaken the man, one beheld in him the very resemblance of the face and exclaimed: "He has come, the one who is like the great stone face!" By constantly beholding the face and meditating upon its majesty, he had grown to look and to be it.

Dear Christian reader, I am sure it is your desire to be Christ-like, to bear the image of Jesus Christ among men. This is the purpose of worship, both in private and in public. The design of worship is that we might grow in grace and that the image of Christ might grow in us. You need no man-made images to assist you in your worship. The plain preaching and teaching of the Word of God is sufficient to bring you into conformity to God's perfect will for your life. Read and study your Bible daily and obediently, and attend places where living messages are delivered for your edification and growth in grace. "And as we have borne the image of the earthly, we shall also bear the image of the heavenly" (1 Cor. 15:49).

CHAPTER IV

THE SACREDNESS OF SPEECH

THE THIRD COMMANDMENT

"Thou shalt not take the name of the Lord thy God in vain; for the Lord will not hold him guiltless that taketh His name in vain" (Exod. 20: 7)

CHAPTER IV

THE SACREDNESS OF SPEECH

"Thou shalt not take the name of the Lord thy God in vain; for the Lord will not hold him guiltless that taketh His name in vain" (Exod. 20: 7).

TWO of the ten commandments deal expressly with the sins of the tongue. In the third commandment God forbids man to speak anything that so much as reflects irreverence toward His Name. In the ninth commandment He said: "Thou shalt not bear false witness against thy neighbor." Thereby He endeavors to protect our name. Often we hear it asked: "What's in a name?" Perhaps there is little or no meaning in some of our names, but God has a sense of the dignity and sacredness of His own Name, and He demands that we be concerned with the honor of the Name of God. Hence He issued the warning against its misuse.

1. A SACRED REVELATION

Man is indebted to God for the revelation of Himself in His Name. At least, the ancient Jews felt so, for they hallowed and regarded the Name of God above all else. We are told that when the scribes copied the sacred manuscripts, the name of God was approached in holy awe and reverence. The penman would stop, bathe himself all over, and return to his

51

desk with a new, hitherto-unused pen. Then he would proceed to write the name *God* in whatever form it appeared. We have lost most of the sacred respect for God's Name. There are any number of men who would fight for the honor of the name of a wife or mother, but many of these same men are utterly indifferent and careless blasphemers who thoughtlessly profane the Name of Almighty God.

What the telescope is to the scientist the Name of God is to His children. Throughout the Bible there are various appellations of God by which we may look into His infinite nature and Person. We name our children for the purpose of identification, but the Names of God in the Bible are descriptive of His nature. A study of this is an excellent approach to a knowledge of His majestic personality and mighty character. Names are revealing, and we can learn much truth in tracing the origin of them. It is a wonderful revelation to the Christian when he hears for the first time the vast amount of truth that is given in connection with the many Names of God. Undoubtedly much of the careless misuse of God's Name can be attributed to the lack of understanding of what the Creator had in His own mind when He first revealed it.

It has been stated that there are more than three hundred Names of God in the Bible. A consideration of the more familiar of these will aid us greatly in our understanding and appreciation of the One with whom we have to do.

The first verse in the Bible tells us, "In the beginning *God* created the heaven and the earth" (Gen. 1: 1). This is the most common Name for Deity in the Old

Testament, appearing well over two thousand times. It is the primary Name of "Elohim," and literally means "The Strong Faithful One." Its appearance is usually associated with the thought of creation, and it testifies of the power of God. It was the "Strong One" who said: "Let Us make man in Our image, after Our likeness" (Gen. 1: 26). We, then, who are the creatures of the mighty One would do well to ponder the strength of Him whose Name is so lightly esteemed among men.

Again, God chose Names to manifest Himself to His people. When the time was ripe for Israel to have a revelation of the Eternal, Self-existing One, then it was that God gave them another of His wonderful Names. It is the Name *Jehovah*, appearing sometimes as LORD or GOD (notice, all capital letters). It is the Name used by God in the first commandment where He said: "I am the LORD thy God." The Name Jehovah is said to be a combination of three Hebrew words which may be translated into an English form as follows:

Yehi—future tense, meaning "He will be."
Hove—present tense, meaning "being, or He that is."
hahyAH—past tense, meaning "He was."

This Name was revealed first to Moses in the flaming bush in Midian where God said: "I AM."

William A. Dean has pointed out the three characteristics of Jehovah that are clearly seen in the Old Testament:

He is the God of holiness (Exod. 15: 11).
He hates and judges sin (Gen. 6: 3-7).
He loves and saves sinners (Exod. 34: 6; Gen. 3: 8,9).

Were it not for this wonderful revelation of God in these Names, His eternality, majesty, fierceness, and love for sinners would not have been so vividly portrayed to Israel. Yet in our modern literature, both fact and fiction, the Names LORD and GOD are often used in blasphemy as well as in other irreverent ways. A knowledge of what God's Name implies and teaches will set a guard upon the lips of all who use that Name.

There came the time when God wanted His people to know that they had but one Master, and this revelation He made known to them in His Name. So we see the Lordship and Mastery of the Creator over His creatures in the Name *Lord*, not to be confused with LORD. It is the word "Adonai," and means *master*. In Scripture the name is used of man as well as of Deity, but where it is so used it never is spelled with large letters, always *lord*. The children of Heth called Abraham *lord*, which word always refers to man (Gen. 23:6). "Moses said unto the LORD, O my Lord" (Exod. 4:10), thereby making a direct reference to Deity. The name *Adonai* was used by the Hebrews to indicate the relationship of a master to his slave. When God wanted to teach Israel that He had a right to absolute obedience from His own children, He used the Name Adonai. Isaiah's obedience to the heavenly call came from Adonai. The prophet said: "I heard the voice of the *Lord*, saying, Whom shall I send, and who will go for us?" It was the voice of the Master asking for the response of obedience. Then Isaiah answered: "Here am I; send me" (Isa. 6:8). Whenever the Name *Lord* is used lightly or disrespectfully, it is a violation of the third commandment. **Men** everywhere need a solemn warning against the misuse of this sacred Name of God, for the day is sure to come when "every knee should bow . . . and every tongue should confess that Jesus Christ is Lord (*Adonai*), to the glory of God the Father" (Phil. 2:11).

Once again, in revealing Himself to man God takes the Name "Most High God." It is the Hebrew Name "El Elyon," and has the thought of ownership. The "Most High God" is the Possessor of heaven and earth. God would teach us here that His authority is not confined to the sphere of the heavenlies. The revelation of God's ownership in His Name was given for the first time to Abraham after he had conquered the enemy kings and delivered Lot. Abraham had brought back much goods from the battle; and lest he should become wrapped up in his possessions and forget God, it was necessary for the Lord to show him that He was Divine Owner of all. The prophet Isaiah spoke of God's heavenly authority when, quoting Satan's boast, he said: "I will ascend above the heights of the clouds; I will be like the *Most High*" (Isa. 14:14). Moses testified to the earthly authority of El Elyon when he said: "The *Most High* divided to the nations their inheritance" (Deut. 32:8). How foolish man becomes when he misuses or abuses the Name of Him on whom each of us is dependent in this life as well as in the life to come.

Again, God revealed Himself in His Name "Almighty God." It was to Abraham also that God made known Himself in this way. The Hebrew word is *El Shaddai*, and means "the All-Sufficient One." When Abraham was ninety-nine years of age God appeared to him, and said: "I am the *Almighty God*" (Gen. 17:1). God here revealed Himself as the Giver and Sustainer of life. From every human observation Abraham was well past the possibility of becoming a father, and still Isaac was yet to be born. In order to convince Abraham that this was not beyond the realm of divine accomplishment God had first to reveal Himself as the Giver and Sustainer of life. As the *Almighty God* He was able to say: "I will make thee exceeding fruitful, and I will make nations of thee, and kings shall come out of thee" (Gen. 17:6). A profane age is unmindful of how seriously it is infringing upon the third commandment in its flippant exclamations of the Name *Almighty God*. Recently I heard a woman in a rage of disappointment, say: "God Almighty!" That was taking the Name of the Lord in vain, and the Lord will not hold him guiltless who takes His name in vain.

These are but a few of the Names used by God to allow man to look into the Divine nature. The dignity with which God regards His holy Name can be seen in the standard which He has erected to defend it. Isaiah listened to the seraphic choristers cry in heavenly harmony, "Holy, holy, holy, is the Lord of hosts." They seemed to be living for the purpose of testifying to His greatness and of hallowing His worthy Name. Elsewhere the prophet quotes God as saying: "I am the LORD: that is My Name: and My glory will I not give to another, neither My praise to graven images" (Isa. 42:8).

In "The Prayer Perfect" Dr. Rimmer has pointed out that the Name of God is hallowed by His entire creation, with the exception of two limited spheres. They are the demons and rebellious sons of Adam.

"Devils, fallen angels, and sinful men form the coalition which seeks to usurp the authority of God and defame His Holy Name."

The Name of God is holy, because it is His revelation of Himself. Therefore we can never separate the Name from the One who bears it. In governmental circles we respect such names as those of Washington and Lincoln. In the sphere of Christianity we love the names of Spurgeon, Moody, Sunday, and others. If the names of these men are revered among us for their integrity and steadfastness, how much more should we approach the Name of God with humility and holy awe.

2. A SOLEMN RESPONSIBILITY

If the Titles of God enhance the revelation of Himself, they likewise enjoin a responsibility upon men. God plainly states that we may not take the Name of the Lord our God in vain. Any loose or frivolous use of His Holy Name will invoke divine judgment upon us. And yet this is a common and a frequent habit that is attaching its tendrils to our American people.

Taking the Name of the Lord in vain is being done in at least three ways—by *profanity, puerility,* and *pretence.*

Profanity is a treacherous practice that prevails among many people. All who are guilty of profanity are classed as profane, and profane persons are irreverent toward God, unholy, and worldly. Swearing is common, even in our home-life in America, and often children are heard using an extensive profane vocabulary which was learned from parents. There are vast numbers of persons, both men and women, who have developed a proficiency in swearing. The vocabularies of some would-be great persons are so impoverished that they have undertaken to fill in their script with profanity. This is obviously true in literature, on the stage, and on the radio. But such a vulgar habit is a strong symptom of an inner disease for, "Out of the abundance of the heart the mouth speaketh" (Matt. 12:34). The sin of swearing is essentially vulgar and loathsome. It is characteristic of the drunkard and the criminal. A survey has shown that in our asylums for idiots and imbeciles it is a painful thing to see the ease and liberty with which the inmates use profanity. Swearing is resorted to by children on the streets, parents in the homes, and by our young people in high schools and colleges. It is a sad commentary on our social life. It is a desecration and debasement of God's creative gift of speech. Cursing and swearing are violent abuses of the goodness of God, and only those who deny Jesus Christ engage themselves in these evil habits. We are not surprised that Peter, in a moment of weakness, denied Christ, and then "began to curse and to swear, saying, I know not this man of whom ye speak" (Mark 14:71). Peter never practised cursing and swearing in the presence of our Lord. It was an old habit of the fisherman before he became a follower of Christ. But Peter's neglect of his spiritual life caused him to fall back into his old habit. When one is in close communion with his Lord he will love and respect that Name which is above every name. He will sing:

> "Jesus, I love Thy charming Name,
>   'Tis music to my ear;
> Fain would I sound it out so loud
>   That heaven and earth might hear."

Puerility is triviality. To be puerile is to be frivolous, and not one of us will attempt to deny that God's Holy Name is often flippantly and even jokingly used. Humorous stories are sometimes told in which the Name of God or Jesus Christ is used to bring forth laughter. This is another way of taking the Lord's Name in vain, and is therefore a violent offense against the third commandment. Sacrilege is the sin of violating or profaning sacred things, and any use of God's Name other than in lowly reverence and holy regard is a sacrilegious act, and "should be shunned as men would shun the fires of Hell." Our Lord delivered a mighty discourse on the destiny of words. Among other challenging statements, He said: "But I say unto you, That every idle word that men shall speak, they shall give account thereof in the day of judgment. For by thy words thou shalt be justified, and by thy words thou shalt be condemned" (Matt. 12: 36, 37). This is a searching saying, and calls for deep thought. Words are not as trifling and unimportant as we sometimes think. One day we will have to give an account of our *words* as well as of our *works*. "A profane scoff or atheistical jest may stick in the minds of those that hear it, after the tongue that spake it is dead. A word spoken is physically transient, but morally permanent."

The writer had a sad experience not long ago at a Bible Conference. Almost two hundred young people had gathered in the assembly hall for an evening service. The afternoon had been given over to recreation, and everyone seemed to be having a good time, including the writer. And I suppose that some of the frivolity was still present when we gathered for the devotional service. The song leader had announced the opening hymn and then called upon me to sing a stanza. Not having been endowed with the gift of singing, I assumed that a prank was being played on me. However, standing on a chair, I proceeded to do my part imitating a lisping boy. The hymn chosen was entitled: "What Can Wash Away My Sins?" When I came to the phrase, "Nothing but the Blood of *Jesus*", a cold chill swept over the audience, for it was evident that such levity had grieved the Holy Spirit. I was making sport of the Name of Jesus, and it cut my own heart to the quick. I was guilty of taking my Lord's Name in vain. Let us be watchful and set a guard over our tongues, for "death and life are in the power of the tongue" (Prov. 18:21).

Finally, let us consider *pretence* as the third way of breaking this commandment. In short, pretence is a lie. Truth-telling is far removed from some people. And how blasphemous it is when, by pretended piety, we call upon God to witness to the truthfulness of what we have said! We look for a measure of pretence from a certain clan of worldling, but certainly not from the children of God. And yet professing Christians are guilty of lying while they appear to be worshipping God. Dr. Morgan has said: "The profanity of the church is infinitely worse than the profanity of the street. The blasphemy of the sanctuary is a far more insidious form of evil than the blasphemy of the slum." If truth is not behind the worship of a man, that man is guilty of taking the Name of the Lord in vain. The breaking of this law takes on its most awful and ugly form in hypocrisy, and of this we must be charged when we pretend to be what we are not.

Our Lord concluded "The Sermon On The Mount" with a strong warning—"Not every one that saith unto Me, Lord, Lord, shall enter into the kingdom of heaven" (Matt. 7: 21).   This teaching of Christ is closely akin to that of the third commandment.   It is a matter of the right and the wrong use of the Lord's Name.   We may use that Name in songs of praise, in prayer, and even in preaching; but if there is any insincerity in us, if our profession does not measure up to our practices, then we have broken the law more frequently than the man who utters an occasional curse. This is a serious offence, and we fear that the day of judgment will bring to light much hypocrisy that passed as pious worship.   How solemn and how sad that day will be for those false prophets in many of our pulpits who utter God's Name in their discourses and yet deny His sovereignty and mutilate His Holy Word!   Oh, the awful judgment that awaits such satanic sects as those who call themselves "Jehovah's Witnesses" but deny the Deity of Jesus Christ, the personality of the Holy Spirit, and kindred truths of God's Word that are essential to eternal life! This common sin of taking the Lord's Name in vain is a serious offence, "For the LORD will not hold him guiltless that taketh His Name in vain."

The application of this truth to the Christian is far-reaching.   Speech is sacred.   "It is the vehicle of the invisible soul, the most spiritual, non-material function of the body."   Therefore, "let your speech be alway with grace, seasoned with salt" (Col. 4: 6), for words are often more forceful than deeds.

"Boys flying kites haul in their white-winged birds;
But you can't do that when you're flying words."

"But now ye also put off all these; . . . filthy communi-
cation out of your mouth. Lie not one to another"
(Col. 3:8, 9). "The tongue is a fire, a world of iniquity
. . . set on fire of hell . . . it is an unruly evil, full of
deadly poison" (James 3: 6, 8).

Let our speech glorify the matchless Name of *Jesus*
always. His is the Name into which "God has com-
pressed His heart, His power, His love." We sing,

> *"The Name of Jesus is so sweet,*
> *I love its music to repeat,"*

and rightly so! "Ye are justified in the Name of the
Lord Jesus" (1 Cor. 6:11). "Repentance and remission of sins should be preached in His Name" (Luke
24: 47). His Name will be our glorious adornment in
Heaven, for, "They shall see His face; and His Name
shall be in their foreheads" (Rev. 22: 4).

> *"Take the Name of Jesus with you,*
> *Child of sorrow and of woe;*
> *It will joy and comfort give you,*
> *Take it, then, where'er you go.*

> *"At the Name of Jesus bowing,*
> *Falling prostrate at His feet,*
> *King of kings in Heav'n we'll crown Him,*
> *When our journey is complete."*

THE SABBATH DAY

The Fourth Commandment

"Remember the sabbath day, to keep it holy. Six days shalt thou labor, and do all thy work: but the seventh day is the sabbath of the LORD thy God: in it thou shalt not do any work, thou, nor thy son, nor thy daughter, thy manservant, nor thy maidservant, nor thy cattle, nor thy stranger that is within thy gates: for in six days the LORD made heaven and earth, the sea, and all that in them is, and rested the seventh day: wherefore the LORD blessed the sabbath day, and hallowed it" (Exod. 20: 8-11).

CHAPTER V

THE SABBATH DAY

"Remember the sabbath day, to keep it holy. Six days shalt thou labor, and do all thy work: but the seventh day is the sabbath of the LORD thy God: in it thou shalt not do any work, thou, nor thy son, nor thy daughter, thy manservant, nor thy maidservant, nor thy cattle, nor thy stranger that is within thy gates: for in six days the LORD made heaven and earth, the sea, and all that in them is, and rested the seventh day: wherefore the LORD blessed the sabbath day, and hallowed it"

(Exod. 20: 8-11).

THE Sabbath question is perhaps one of the most misunderstood today. The problem is not new. The sect known as "Seventh Day Adventists" are in reality the descendants of the Pharisees of our Lord's day. But even among well-meaning professing Christians there is confusion regarding the fourth commandment. However, the worst danger lies among those who hold that keeping the Sabbath is the sum and substance of all righteousness, and that breaking the Sabbath is the sum of all evil. There is need for the study of God's Word on this subject so that we might know what the Holy Spirit teaches about the Sabbath question.

1. THE SABBATH IN THE OLD TESTAMENT

Before studying the purposes of the Sabbath, it will help us if we have fixed in our minds just what the word "Sabbath" means. The word "Sabbath" means literally *cessation*, or *rest*, and it has a peculiar reference to one resting from labor. The day set apart in the fourth commandment was to be observed as a day of rest from all secular work. The Bible teaches clearly that Saturday, the seventh day, always was and always will be a Sabbath day.

The first time we find mentioned the seventh day as a Sabbath is in connection with the work of God in creation. We read:

"Thus the heavens and the earth were finished, and all the host of them. And on the seventh day God ended His work which He had made; and He rested on the seventh day from all His work which He had made. And God blessed the seventh day, and sanctified it: because that in it He had rested from all His work which God created and made" (Gen. 2: 1-3).

We find no commandment given to man here. It merely is stated that God finished all the work He wanted to accomplish in six days, and that on the seventh day He rested from His work. The teaching here is two-fold: "cessation from work, and satisfaction with the work." The task was done and done well within six days, so on the seventh day God rested. Later on God saw to it that the Israelites observed the seventh day as a rest day before the law was given to Moses on Mount Sinai. When God sent them manna, He instructed them to gather twice as much on the sixth day and added: "Tomorrow is the rest of the holy sabbath unto the Lord" (Exod. 16: 22, 23). Not all the people obeyed, for we are told "that there went out some of the people on the seventh day for to

gather." God called Moses again and instructed him
to "let no man go out of his place on the seventh day,"
the result being "the people rested on the seventh day"
(Exod. 16: 27-30). It is clear from these two passages
that God required from man that one day out of
seven be devoted to rest.

From the creation of Adam work has been assigned
to man. Before the fall Adam was responsible to keep
and dress the garden. After the fall the ground was
cursed, and man's labor became more strenuous. It is
evident that the will of God for man is that he should
work. Following God's curse upon the ground, He
said: "In sorrow (or toil) shalt thou eat of it all the
days of thy life" (Gen. 3: 17).

Though God appointed man to work, He called him
to worship as well. If man would concern himself with
the physical only, then the spiritual would be neglected.
No man can concentrate on that which is earthly to the
neglect of the heavenly. As Dr. Morgan has said:
"In every hour of human life the physical and the
spiritual interact upon each other, and in their proper
inter-relation each contributes to the strengthening of
the other." When we give ourselves entirely to meeting
the needs of the body and satisfying the desires of
the flesh, the soul is certain to become impoverished.
To gain the whole world and lose one's soul is to lose
all. Therefore, many years before the Law was given
at Sinai, God set aside a period of time in which man
was to cease from his labors and worship God. Furthermore, it is clear that the time to be consecrated for
the rest of the body and the exercise of the soul was
one day out of seven. However, it is nowhere implied
that any Sabbath law was enjoined upon man during

that period of history from Adam to Moses. As a law the Sabbath was not enforced upon man until God gave it to Israel on Sinai.

More than ninety times in the Old Testament and more than fifty times in the New Testament, Saturday, the seventh day of the week, is referred to as the Sabbath Day. From this teaching we can conclude that the seventh day, or Saturday, was always a Sabbath or rest day. However, we must be careful to notice that while Saturday is always a Sabbath, the Sabbath is not always a Saturday. In the Old Testament, even after the Mosaic Law was given, there are instances of the Sabbath occurring on other days. When we study the Feasts of Jehovah, we are told that the Feast of Trumpets was to be observed on the first day of the seventh month. "The Lord spake unto Moses, saying, Speak unto the children of Israel, saying, In the seventh month, in the first day of the month, shall ye have a Sabbath, a memorial of blowing of trumpets, an holy convocation. Ye shall do no servile work therein: but ye shall offer an offering made by fire unto the Lord" (Lev. 23:23-26). Here, then, we have a yearly Sabbath, a day of rest and worship once each year. But it is apparent immediately that this Sabbath will not fall on Saturday in two consecutive years.

Again the Lord spoke to Moses relative to commemorating the Feast of Tabernacles—"Speak unto the children of Israel, saying, The fifteenth day of this seventh month shall be the feast of tabernacles for seven days unto the Lord" (Lev. 23:34). The feast was to be kept for seven days, and "on the first day shall be a sabbath, and on the eighth day shall be a sabbath" (Ver. 39). There is no problem, therefore, when we conclude that other days were called Sabbaths by God besides the seventh day of the week.

We find further that the Law of Rest was not confided solely to man. There was a governmental Law of Rest that applied to the physical universe as well. It was God's law of agriculture that provided for a period of rest for the whole land once every seven years. The land could be plowed, sown, and reaped for six consecutive years; but during the seventh year the land was not to be worked at all. This was the divinely arranged method for conserving the productivity of the soil. Science has long since agreed that there is less chance of the ground being depleted of its natural resources if nothing is taken out of it for one season at least. This law given by God is as follows:

"And the LORD spake unto Moses in mount Sinai, saying, Speak unto the children of Israel, and say unto them, When ye come into the land which I give you, then shall the land keep a sabbath unto the LORD. Six years thou shalt sow thy field, and six years thou shalt prune thy vineyard, and gather in the fruit thereof; but in the seventh year shall be a sabbath of rest unto the land, a sabbath for the LORD: thou shalt neither sow thy field, nor prune thy vineyard. That which groweth of its own accord of thy harvest thou shalt not reap, neither gather the grapes of thy vine undressed: for it is a year of rest unto the land. And the sabbath of the land shall be meat for you; for thee, and for thy servant, and for thy maid, and for thy hired servant, and for thy stranger that sojourneth with thee, and for thy cattle, and for the beast that are in thy land, shall all the increase thereof be meat. And thou shalt number seven sabbaths of years unto thee, seven times seven years;

and the space of the seven sabbaths of years shall be
unto thee forty and nine years. . . . Wherefore ye shall do
my statutes, and keep my judgments, and do them; and ye
shall dwell in the land in safety. And the land shall yield
her fruit, and ye shall eat your fill, and dwell therein in
safety. And if ye shall say, What shall we eat the seventh year? behold, we shall not sow, nor gather in our
increase: then I will command My blessing upon you in
the sixth year, and it shall bring forth fruit for three
years. And ye shall sow the eighth year, and eat yet of
old fruit until the ninth year; until her fruits come in
ye shall eat of the old store" (Lev. 25: 1-8, 18-22).

The teaching in the above passage is plain. Each
seventh year was a Sabbath (or rest) year for the
land. It was not to be plowed nor planted, and the
people were guaranteed that there would never be
over-production nor famine. If they believed God
and obeyed His command, they would have sufficient
to meet every need. But Israel, instead of obeying God,
ignored His command and greedily worked the ground
in the Sabbath year. The sad result was that Palestine,
once the world's most fertile and fruitful spot, became
barren and fruitless. The disobedience of the people
brought upon them one of the worst disasters in Jewish
history. For *seventy* years Israel was held in Babylon-
ian captivity. It is an interesting and instructive fact
that from the time Israel entered the Land until she
was led away captive was four hundred and ninety
(490) years. If the land had been given its Rest
Year in every seven, it would have lain idle for seventy
years. Therefore, God took them out of the Land and
permitted their captivity for exactly seventy years, one
year for each Sabbath Year they failed to observe in
the Land. God had said:

"And I will bring the land into desolation: and your enemies which dwell therein shall be astonished at it. And I will scatter you among the heathen, and will draw out a sword after you: and your land shall be desolate, and your cities waste. Then shall the land enjoy her sabbaths, as long as it lieth desolate, and ye be in your enemies' land; even then shall the land rest, and enjoy her sabbaths. As long as it lieth desolate it shall rest; because it did not rest in your sabbaths, when ye dwelt upon it" (Lev. 26: 32-35).

How exact are His commands, and how righteous His judgments! The Word of God is not to be tampered with or disobeyed. To do so will bring sure judgment upon him who violates the Holy Laws contained in it.

It is important that we observe at this point that the Sabbath, *as a law,* is distinctly a Jewish institution. The Ten Commandments are prefaced by the voice of God saying: "I am the LORD thy God, which have brought thee out of the land of Egypt."

We read further where God said:

"Keep the sabbath day to sanctify it, as the LORD thy God hath commanded thee. Six days thou shalt labor, and do all thy work: but the seventh day is the sabbath of the LORD thy God: in it thou shalt not do any work, thou, nor thy son, nor thy daugher, nor thy manservant, nor thy maidservant, nor thine ox, nor thine ass, nor any of thy cattle, nor thy stranger that is within thy gates; that thy manservant and thy maidservant may rest as well as thou. And remember that thou wast a servant in the land of Egypt, and that the LORD thy God brought thee out thence through a mighty hand and by a stretched out arm: therefore the LORD thy God commanded thee to keep the sabbath day"
(Deut. 5: 12-15).

Again God said to Moses: "Speak thou also unto the children of Israel, saying, Verily My Sabbaths *ye* shall keep" (Exod. 31: 13).

The prophet Ezekiel quotes God as saying:

"Wherefore I caused them to go forth out of the land of Egypt, and brought them into the wilderness. . . . Moreover also I gave them My Sabbaths, to be a sign between Me and them" (Ezek. 20: 10, 12).

The Old Testament Scriptures concerning the Sabbath cannot be applied to the Gentiles *as a law*, for it was Israel's relationship to the Law that distinguished her from all other peoples of the earth. Furthermore, the fourth commandment is the only one of the ten that is not reiterated or reaffirmed in the New Testament, and not one verse will be found that makes the Sabbath binding upon the Christian. However, the more general application of Sabbath truth is sadly neglected in our day. Proper physical rest for the body is given little consideration, and much less thought is given to the spiritual development of the soul. Greed and the gratification of lustful desires are mastering the majority of the people in the world today. Even among professing Christians there is little time and thought devoted to the things of God and the cause of Jesus Christ.

If God deemed it wise to set apart from the time of creation one day out of seven for rest and worship, certainly we are making a sad mistake when we push agriculture, industry, and our own bodies beyond the ability to produce well. The shame of industry is that it presses and oppresses the laborer. The shame of the laborer, the Christian included, is that he refuses to be satisfied with God's plan for everyday living. The cry of the average person is that "it will never work." If that is so, then God erred greatly when He issued these instructions. I agree that God's economy will never be adopted in this age. I am not looking for the world to turn to the obedience of God's Word in this age; but I am sure that these laws, designed for those who would live righteously, will work perfectly when Jesus sets up His Millennial Kingdom on earth.

There is yet a time future when Israel will be restored as a nation, and in God's dealings with her as such, the Law of the Sabbath which she wilfully violated, will be restored also. God has said: "For as the new heavens and the new earth, which I will make, shall remain before Me, saith the Lord, so shall your seed and your name remain. And it shall come to pass, that from one sabbath to another, shall all flesh come to worship before Me, saith the Lord" (Isa. 66: 22, 23). "Likewise the people of the land shall worship at the door of this gate before the Lord in the sabbaths and in the new moons" (Eze. 46: 3). The Old Testament Law of the Sabbath as given expressly to Israel has been temporarily laid aside during the times of the Gentiles and the Church Age. But when Christ returns to catch up the Church to meet Him in the air, the times of the Gentiles will have been fulfilled, and once again God will deal with Israel, and the Sabbath will become a Jewish institution in that day.

2. THE SABBATH IN THE NEW TESTAMENT

We have said that no question caused so much strife and contention among the religious leaders of our Lord's day as the question of the Sabbath. When constantly pressing the Sabbath question to Christ and His disciples, the Pharisees were straining at a gnat; for they gave every evidence of not understanding the correct interpretation of the Sabbath.

We stated also that the fourth commandment is the one of the Ten Commandments that is not reaffirmed in the New Testament. The Apostle Paul wrote: "Owe no man anything, but to love one another: for he that loveth another hath fulfilled the law. For this, Thou shalt not commit adultery, Thou shalt not kill, Thou shalt not steal, Thou shalt not bear bear false witness, Thou shalt not covet; and if there be any other commandment, it is briefly comprehended in this saying, namely, Thou shalt love thy neighbor as thyself. Love worketh no ill to his neighbor: therefore love is the fulfilling of the law" (Rom. 13: 8-10). Commenting on this passage, Dr. Torrey has said: "Here five commandments are reaffirmed, not because they were given by Moses, but because they grow out of the law of love, which is the law of Christ." The command to "honor thy father and thy mother" is reaffirmed in Paul's Epistle to the Ephesians where he said: "Children, obey your parents in the Lord: for this is right. Honor thy father and mother; which is the first commandment with promise" (Eph. 6: 1, 2). In the Epistle of James we have a reiteration of the command not to take the Name of the Lord in vain—"But above all things, my brethren, swear not, neither by heaven, neither by earth, neither by any other oath: but let your yea be yea; and your nay, nay; lest ye fall into condemnation" (James 5: 12). An affirmation of the first and second commandments is given us by John when he said: "Little children, keep yourselves from idols" (1 John 5: 21). Nine commandments, then, are seen in the New Testament to enjoin a definite responsibility upon Christians, but nowhere is the same truth stated or implied as far as the fourth commandment is concerned.

Are we to conclude, therefore, that there is no responsibility at all resting upon believers in regard to a day of rest and worship? To the contrary, every child of God owes the world, as well as his Lord and himself, a debt of gratitude for what Jesus Christ has accomplished for him on the ground of divine grace. However, we must exercise great care and caution so as not to confuse the Sabbath Day, as set forth in the New Testament, with the Day that is recognized by the Christian Church as the Day of rest and worship.

It seems a necessity to state here that our Lord Jesus Christ observed no other day during His life on earth than Saturday, the seventh day of the week, the Jewish Sabbath. Jesus in the flesh was a Jew, David's Son, of the tribe of Judah, and as such He was under obligation to keep the Law of Moses. As a Hebrew of the Hebrews, Jesus obeyed and enforced the Law of the Sabbath as a vital and an integral part of the entire Mosaic Law. We are told explicitly that He was "made under the law" (Gal. 4: 4), and also that He "was a minister of the circumcision for the truth of God" (Rom. 15: 8). Christ Himself said: "Think not that I am come to destroy the law, or the prophets: I am come not to destroy, but to fulfill" (Matt. 5: 17). This was the voice of a greater than Moses, even the Divine Lawgiver Himself. He had the authority to abolish the Sabbath or to change it as He chose, for "He said unto them, That the Son of Man is Lord also of the Sabbath" (Luke 6:5). Though Christ was unjustly criticized for breaking the Law of the Sabbath, He kept it perfectly all the days of His earthly life, even though He claimed to be superior to that day.

On one occasion our Lord "went through the corn fields on the Sabbath day; and His disciples began, as they went, to pluck the ears of corn. And the Pharisees said unto Him, Behold, why do they on the Sabbath day that which is not lawful?" (Mark 2:23, 24.) The Pharisees were always on hand that they might find some fault with the Lord Jesus, and they were quick to seize upon this opportunity to condemn His disciples for plucking corn on the Sabbath. Jesus answered them that "The Sabbath was made for man, and not man for the Sabbath."

When God instituted the Sabbath, He did it for man's benefit; it was appointed for man's well-being. He made it for the good of man's body and soul. Therefore it was never to become a burden to him, but a blessing instead. The Sabbath was never intended to prevent an act of mercy, but to bring happiness to man. The sanctity of the Sabbath day lies in the fact that it was made to minister to the needs of man. "It retains its sanctity as it serves man."

THE END OF THE SABBATH

We have seen the place that God intended the Sabbath should have in the life of Israel, but it is important that we know when these Jewish observances were to cease. The prophet Hosea recorded God as saying: "I will also cause all her mirth to cease, her feast days, her new moons, and her sabbaths, and all her solemn feasts" (Hosea 2:11). It is clear that when judgment would fall upon Israel, along with other forms of chastisement, her Sabbaths would cease.

When was this prophecy fulfilled? We do not hesitate to declare emphatically that the cross of Calvary, the death of our Lord and Saviour Jesus Christ, was the termination of Jewish Law. Having kept the Law fully, its penalty of death for violation was removed from Him. More than this: every sinner that receives Jesus Christ as Substitute and Saviour is likewise delivered from the curse of a broken Law, for by His sacrificial death He paid in full for all the sins of every man—"Christ is the end of the Law for righteousness to every one that believeth" (Rom. 10:4). The whole of the Mosaic system, including the Ten Commandments, has given way completely to this age of sovereign grace. The Sabbath day is done away in the cross of Christ. The Apostle Paul said: "Let no man therefore judge you in meat, or in drink, or in respect of an holyday, or of the new moon, or of the sabbath days: which are a shadow of things to come; but the body (or the substance) is of Christ" (Col. 2:16, 17). Our Lord Jesus is the Substance, therefore we need not cling any longer to the shadow, for we have been delivered from the curse and the bondage of the Sabbath day.

HAS THE CHRISTIAN ANY RESPONSIBILITY?

When the Bible teaches that the Ten Commandments are done away in the death of Christ on the cross, it does not so much as imply that the Christian is left without a code of ethics regarding a day of rest and worship. Though there is no command in the New

Testament given to reverence any one day in the week above another, we do have sufficient teaching to support the first day of the week as the established day for worshipping God. We are not agreeing in the least with those who think that if they go to church on Sunday and piously go through the forms of the service, that they can live for the Devil the rest of the week. Every day is the Lord's Day, and those of us who name the Name of Christ are indebted to His grace to live for Him every day, for His glory and the salvation of lost souls. But we do have the first day of the week (Sunday) at which time we should cease from our labor and give ourselves to God's service. There is nothing in the New Testament to support the oft-misquoted phrase "Christian Sabbath". It is the first day of the week, the Lord's Day, and upon resurrection ground the Christian Church has set it aside for spiritual activity. It is nowhere enjoined upon us as a law, but must be looked upon as the gift of Christ and is therefore a privilege. But woe be to the man or the woman who despises that privilege.

God has set His seal upon the first day of the week as we see in the following passages:

"And very early in the morning the first day of the week, they came unto the sepulchre at the rising of the sun" (Mark 16: 2).

"Now when Jesus was risen early the first day of the week, He appeared first to Mary Magdalene, out of whom He had cast seven devils" (Mark 16: 9).

"Now upon the first day of the week, very early in the morning, they came unto the sepulchre, bringing the spices which they had prepared, and certain others with them. And they found the stone rolled away from the sepulchre. And they entered in, and found not the body of the Lord Jesus" (Luke 24: 1-3).

"Then the same day at evening, being the first day of the week, when the doors were shut where the disciples were assembled for fear of the Jews, came Jesus and stood in the midst, and saith unto them, Peace be unto you" (John 20: 19).

"And upon the first day of the week, when the disciples came together to break bread, Paul preached unto them, ready to depart on the morrow; and continued his speech until midnight" (Acts 20: 7).

"Upon the first day of the week let every one of you lay by him in store, as God hath prospered him, that there be no gatherings when I come" (1 Cor. 16: 2).

"I was in the Spirit on the Lord's day, and heard behind me a great voice, as of a trumpet (Rev. 1: 10).

Sunday is Christ's gift to His Church. You may receive it or reject it. We are on resurrection ground when we avail ourselves of the privilege of resting from secular labor and devoting His day for His glory. Do not make yourself miserable by hedging a number of rigid rules about the Lord's Day. It is a day of joy and gladness. When Jesus appeared to His disciples on that first Easter Sunday, John says: "Then were the disciples glad when they saw the Lord" (John 20: 19, 20). Sunday should be the most joyful day in the week, but for many it is the most hectic and disconcerting.

Dr. Chappell has said: "It is the day when we have some of our biggest athletic contests. It is the day when many, even of our church-people, give their most elaborate parties. It is the day for our biggest picnics. It is the day on which we try to get enough exercise to last us an entire week, when we try to get enough sunburn to take a full six days to heal. It is the day when the largest crowds flock to our theaters. It is the day when our roads are most congested by traffic. It is the day that we send the greatest number of wounded to our hospitals. It is the day on which we send the largest number of slaughtered to our morgues." It is all true! But the half has not been told. The desecration of the Lord's Day is doubtless one of the gross sins of Christendom. O Christian awake!

> "This is the day the Lord hath made;
>   He calls the hours His own:
> Let heaven rejoice, let earth be glad,
>   And praise surround the throne.
> Today He rose and left the dead,
>   And Satan's empire fell;
> Today the saints His triumphs spread,
>   And all His wonders tell."

In closing, I will but suggest to my reader the eternal Sabbath for the redeemed of all ages. The author of the Epistle to the Hebrews has said: "There remaineth therefore a rest (or 'Sabbath rest') to the people of God" (Heb. 4:9, R.V.). The writer of the letter would lead us here into the rest of God. It is the deep, unbroken rest of the soul that we enjoy in measure on earth, but which in the day of His appearing we shall enjoy for evermore. Then it will be a rest from striving and struggling, a rest from the snares of Satan, an unbroken rest that trenscends the loftiest conceptions of our finite minds. Isaiah said, "His rest shall be glorious" (Isa. 11:10). May God speed the day of Christ's return when we shall enter into our eternal rest, "a sabbath-keeping that shall have no end."

CHAPTER VI
THE SAFE-GUARD FOR LIFE

THE FIFTH COMMANDMENT

"Honor thy father and thy mother: that thy
days may be long upon the land which the Lord
thy God giveth thee" (Exod. 20: 12).

THE SAFE-GUARD FOR LIFE

"Honor thy father and thy mother: that thy days may be long upon the land which the Lord thy God giveth thee" (Exod. 20: 12).

THE fifth commandment has been called "the centre-piece of the Decalogue, the keystone of the Sinaitic arch." We commenced the chapter on the first commandment by pointing out that the first four commandments show us man's responsibility toward God, and that the last six commandments deal with man's relationship to his fellow-man. We are aware of the difference of opinion among scholars as to the placing of the fifth commandment. However, the writer believes that the commandment itself deals with the relation of one human being to another, and therefore we have given it place in the second half of the Decalogue.

We re-emphasize here the important truth that right relations with our fellow-men grow out of right relation with God. Until we have applied the truth taught in the first table of the Decalogue, we shall struggle vainly in our efforts to keep the second table with a view to gaining the favor of God. All who enter Heaven's gate will do so by virtue of accepting Jesus Christ as Saviour and Sin-Bearer, and any effort to keep the Law apart from being born again is wasted effort. We remember that Jesus said to a ritualistic observer of the Law, "Except a man be born again, he cannot see the kingdom of God" (John 3:3).

We stress this teaching because we have seen in persons who have not confessed Christ as personal Saviour many fine examples of the virtues found in these commandments. In fact there are non-Christians who put some believers to shame. Some months ago I visited a home where the parents never attend church nor Sunday School. There is not even a Bible in that home. Yet I saw there an example of obedience to parents that one seldom sees in a Christian home. Therefore it is necessary that we do not overlook the fact that the duty enjoined upon us here in the fifth commandment pre-supposes the sovereignty of God in our lives.

1. THE PRECEPT.

The fifth statement of the Decalogue contains a *precept* and a *promise*. It begins with the command from God, saying: "Honor thy father and thy mother."

Shakespeare said: "The voice of parents is the voice of gods, for to their children they are Heaven's lieutenants." Every one of us owes his existence in this world to his parents. Except for them we would not be here. The subsisting relation between parents and children is the very closest, and this keeps the commandment free of any element of unfairness. I once heard it said that the parent is, in a certain sense, the representative of God. It is generally true that upon a child's love and obedience to his parents depends his love and obedience to God in later years. Blessed are those children that pass from a life of obedience to parents to a life of obedience to their heavenly Father.

Think of God's wonderful provision for children in the relationship of parent and child. The needs of a child from infancy demand the greatest care. He must be fed, clothed, and sheltered; and no one in all the world is drawn as instinctively close to a child as are its parents. Every child should be made to see how humbly grateful he should be for the gift of parenthood. Without the God-given parental care and concern we might be maimed or diseased all of our days upon earth. To honor and obey our parents is to submit to a Law of God, given to safe-guard child-life.

Consider the protection of child-life as provided for in parenthood. The mind of a child cannot possibly make accurate decisions or use correct judgment. When our first boy was two years of age he would have opened the car door and stepped out on the highway while I was driving thirty-five miles an hour, were it not for my restraining hand. Having no sense of danger he would instinctively reach for a razor-blade or for rat-poison. Until the mind is sufficiently trained, God has given to every child the mind of its parents as a safe-guard. Children may know the mind of a mother or a father as it is expressed in so many words, and the fifth commandment calls upon every boy and every girl to reverence and obey the wishes of their parents. The precept assumes a superior knowledge on the part of parents over children. Therefore, it is right for children to obey their parents because parents know more than they.

A teacher said to a group of young girl graduates, "You know quite a bit."

"Quite right. You are speaking even more wisely than you realize," they answered.

He continued, "But you do not intend to quit learning. You do not expect to become victims of arrested development. You expect to know far more twenty-five years from now than you know today."

The wise teacher went on, "Since that is the case, it is well for you to remember that your mothers have had just about that much start on you. Therefore, when you get home you might listen to them a bit." *

When children are unwilling to share the knowledge of parents they are acting unwisely. If a small boy insists upon drinking turpentine for water just because he cannot see any difference in the two, he will suffer for it. Parents would act wisely if, when children insist upon pursuing the wrong course, they would take disciplinary measures. It is deadly to allow a child to reach his own conclusions. The man of wisdom has said: "He that spareth his rod hateth his son: but he that loveth him chasteneth him betimes" (Prov. 13: 24). When children are permitted to act apart from parental control they are almost certain to turn from the counsel of God in later years. Strenuous years lie ahead of every child. Choices and decisions will have to be made. The struggles of life will then become a reality. Always it has been men and women who learned to live in obedience to parents who have faced life's issues and emerged victors.

We are told that George Washington had his heart set on going to sea. His trunk was already on board ship when he went to say goodbye to his mother. He

---

* *Ten Rules For Living.*

found her in tears, and with a heavy heart that opposed his going away.

Calling one of the hired men, he said: "Go and tell them to return my trunk. I will not leave and break my mother's heart."

His godly mother took him in her arms and sobbed, saying: "George, God has promised to bless the children that obey their parents. I believe He will bless you." The Church, the State, and society stand or fall according to the family standing. All of human society is closely related to the home. The children we are rearing today are the statesmen, industrialists, farmers, and preachers of tomorrow. If children allow God to govern them now by the hands of their parents, they will find it easier to fit into His plan in years to come.

As we look upon modern civilization in the light of the fifth commandment we must admit that the condition existing is a rotten one. America's biggest problem today is the problem of crime. The Federal Bureau of Investigation reports that juvenile delinquency is our country's growing menace. And to think that these young criminals are coming out of our homes! Our youth are finding it easy to violate the laws of our land simply because they were not disciplined in their homes. When the Apostle Paul predicted the apostasy of the "last days," he warned of the many who would be "disobedient to parents" (2 Tim. 3:2). These he classifies with others whom he calls "blasphemers, fierce, traitors." These evil characteristics fall within the scope of what we call Christendom (professing Christian), for Paul speaks of them as "having a form of godliness, but denying

the power thereof" (2 Tim. 3:5). It is a deadly
evil to ignore this safe-guard given to us by God.

In his First Epistle to Timothy, the Apostle Paul
said: "If any widow have children or nephews, let
them learn first to show piety at home, and to requite
their parents: for that is good and acceptable before
God" (1 Tim. 5:4). Many years ago when God,
Christ, and the Bible were ruled out of Chinese life,
China was the world's finest example of a heathen
nation where parents were obeyed. Even to this day
parental obedience ranks among the leading virtues of
that great nation. How sad to think that here in
America where the gospel has been preached for so
long a time this commandment should be so grossly
abused! The traditions among the ancient peoples of
the world have oftentimes put to shame the Christian
with his spiritual enlightenment. Obedience to parents
is no guarantee that a man will get to Heaven, but
disobedience is a positive sign of a sinful heart without
a knowledge of God. The disobedient sons of Eli were
called "sons of Belial; they knew not the Lord"
(1 Sam. 2:12).

2. THE PROMISE.

The fifth commandment is reaffirmed in the New
Testament in the Epistle to the Ephesians—

"Children, obey your parents in the Lord: for this is
right. Honor thy father and mother; which is the first
commandment with promise; that it may be well with
thee, and thou mayest live long on the earth"
(Eph. 6: 1-3).

Paul is not stating that this is the first commandment, but rather that it is "the first commandment *with promise.*" Here, then, is a promise coupled with the precept. The results of accepting and obeying the commandment will be a personal reward for the one who obeys. "There can be no doubt that the personal element is present, for in the majority of cases the honoring of the parents results in the realization of habits and character that tend to the lengthening of days," says Dr. G. Campbell Morgan. Where there is no parental care, children are apt to eat irregularly and stay up late at nights, as well as to fall into many other habits that lead to poor health, all of which tend to shorten life.

Of course the words of Saint Paul are directed to Christian children, and they teach us one way in which children may exalt the Lord Jesus Christ and at the same time bear a Christian testimony. The matter of obedience is put on the basis of what is right and proper. It is wrong to encourage the practice that a child's will should never be crossed and that every child should be left alone to make its own decisions. The Bible says that children are to "obey." To refuse to obey is a sin that is placed in a list with the most degrading wickedness (Rom. 1: 29-32). The results of disobedience are sad. Not only is the guilty one stripped of the promised reward, but he is a potential inmate for a prison or reformatory, both of which are filled with "spoiled children" who never were taught to obey at home. It is said that the early Romans became excellent citizens and efficient warriors because they learned obedience as children in the home. Little wonder! Does not the promise say: "That it may be well with thee"?

Elsewhere we read: "Children, obey your parents *in all things:* for this is well pleasing unto the Lord" (Col. 3: 20). For Christian children and young people to ignore this principle of obedience, namely, to obey "in all things," is to show forth insubordination to God who gave the command. The son or daughter is commanded to obey without compromise—*in all things.*

Our Lord Jesus Christ is the finest example of implicit obedience. At the age of twelve years He went with His parents to Jerusalem at the feast of the passover. Upon their return "He went down with them, and came to Nazareth, *and was subject unto them*" (Luke 2: 51). On one occasion our Lord, when referring to His heavenly Father, said: "I do *always* those things that please Him" (John 8: 29). We see here how closely linked together are our obedience to God and our obedience to our earthly parents. If, at any time our Lord were disobedient to Mary or Joseph, He would have been guilty of violating the Mosaic Law. But we know that He never once broke away from their restraint.

Truly, divine favor and blessing rest upon all who practise this precept.

"My son, forget not my law; but let thine heart keep My commandments" (Prov. 3: 1).

"For length of days, and long life, and peace, shall they add to thee" (Prov. 3: 2).

"So shalt thou find favor and good understanding in the sight of God and man" (Prov. 3: 4).

In the Book of Jeremiah we have the story of the Rechabites. Because they obeyed the commandment of God in their obedience to Jonadab their father, God promised that the house of Jonadab should stand forever.

"And Jeremiah said unto the house of the Rechabites, Thus saith the Lord of hosts, the God of Israel; Because ye have obeyed the commandment of Jonadab your father, and kept all his precepts, and done according unto all that he hath commanded you: therefore thus saith the Lord of hosts, the God of Israel; Jonadab the son of Rechab shall not want a man to stand before Me for ever" (Jer. 35: 18, 19).

Geikie tells us that the promise has been wonderfully fulfilled, for as late as the year 1862 A.D., Signor Pierotti met a tribe of Rechabites near the south-east end of the Dead Sea. At that time they still were observing the precepts of Jonadab, given in the time of Elijah the Prophet.

"My son, keep thy father's commandment, and forsake not the law of thy mother: bind them continually upon thine heart, and tie them about thy neck. When thou goest, it shall lead thee; when thou sleepest, it shall keep thee; and when thou awakest, it shall talk with thee"
(Prov. 6: 20-22).

But woe to the son or the daughter that refuses to heed the solemn warning!

"The eye that mocketh at his father, and despiseth to obey his mother, the ravens of the valley shall pick it out, and the young eagles shall eat it" (Prov. 30: 17).

Be sure that the judgment of the Lord will not pass over one of you who insists upon disobedience to parents. The case of Absalom, the son of David, is a warning to all. Though possessed of rare beauty, winsome personality, and unusual talents, Absalom died a horrible and painful death. Hanging from the bough of a great oak-tree, pierced through his heart with three of Joab's darts, Absalom warns us against failing to honor our parents. Instead of being buried in a costly mausoleum, Absalom was cast in a grave like a dead dog, leaving behind him a bereaved and brokenhearted father.

O children and young people, give serious thought to this solemn command in God's Word. You cannot afford to trifle with it. If you would enjoy the blessing of God, if you would please God, if you would partake of the promised reward of God, then I exhort you to give prayerful consideration to the instruction of your parents. Honor and reverence your mother and your father. They are God's gift to you—His safe-guard for your life until that day when you have ripened into full manhood and womanhood and are able to face the problems of life.

A final word to parents! Your child should be able to remember the family altar from its earliest childhood. If you would have dutiful children, you cannot afford to shirk your duty as a Christian parent. "Bring them up in the nurture and admonition of the Lord" (Eph. 6: 4). Rule your house well, and respect and love will reign. Cultivate the minds and morals of your children. As Christian parents, keep in mind the well-being of your children and seek to lead them into the truth of God.

The Apostle Paul had the highest commendation to offer Timothy, but Timothy's consecrated life dated back to early childhood. "And that from a child thou hast known the Holy Scriptures, which are able to make thee wise unto salvation through faith which is in Jesus Christ" (2 Tim. 3:15). As we teach our children to depend upon God, the Holy Spirit will make the law of obedience a worth-while reality in their lives. By prayer, by perseverance, by parental love, you may be blessed with the greatest God-given privilege this side of Heaven, namely that of leading your own children to a saving knowledge of the Lord Jesus Christ.

As children of God there is a general application to this commandment found in the Epistle to the Hebrews. "Furthermore we have had fathers of our flesh which corrected us, and we gave them reverence: shall we not much rather be in subjection unto the Father of spirits, and live?" (Heb. 12:9.) Since it is right to obey our earthly fathers whose judgment is imperfect, how much rather ought we to subject ourselves to our heavenly Father, whose wisdom is infallible and whose love is perfect. God's demands and His discipline are but tokens of His constant care and watchfulness. Our whole life must be under His rule and restraint. The chief aim of the parental discipline of our earthly parents is for our earthly future. But the aim of God's restraint upon us is to make us partakers of His holiness. The reward promised for obedience to earthly parents affects us in this life, but the rewards for obedience to our heavenly Father will be ours throughout eternity. Of our Lord it is written: "Though He were a Son, yet learned He obedience" (Heb. 5:8), and we know that He lived in subjection to His Father all of His lifetime, for "He became obedient unto death, even the death of the cross"

(Phil. 2: 8).   Now to us it is written: "Know ye not, that to whom ye yield yourselves servants to obey, his servants ye are to whom ye obey; whether of sin unto death, or of obedience unto righteousness" (Rom. 6: 16).

THE SACREDNESS OF HUMAN LIFE

THE SIXTH COMMANDMENT

"Thou shalt not kill" (Exod. 20: 13).

CHAPTER VII

THE SACREDNESS OF HUMAN LIFE

"Thou shalt not kill" (Exod. 20: 13).

LIFE is a problem! How to live it, and live it well
in the interest of others as well as in the interest
of one's self, has been the unsettled difficulty of the
centuries. With keen interest we have watched the
progress the world has made in an endeavor to pre-
serve life. We marvel at the strides the medical profession has made and at the growing interest of humane
societies. But in spite of all effort on the part of some
to secure and save life, we are amazed with what little
worth and import the world looks at life. When Prince
Clement Metternich, the Austrian statesman, told
Napoleon I that his proposed plan would cost the lives
of one hundred thousand men, the proud emperor only
replied: "A hundred thousand men? What is a hundred thousand men to me?"

Napoleon is but one of millions whose selfish,
avaricious, and revengeful spirit has taken a great toll
of human life. This is due in part, at least, to the dis-
torted views of those who teach that every form and
condition of life, including man, is the direct result of
evolution. Those who postulate an accidental union
of lifeless particles in such a manner that life just
"happened" have a weak presentation of how man first

appeared on the earth. Little wonder that the estimate of human life is so low. The modern juggernaut of evolution has caused men to lose all sense of life's true estimate. But because it cannot stand, even as a hypothesis, we feel that a correct evaluation of life will be approached when we know its real source and substance.

1. THE SOURCE OF HUMAN LIFE.

The Prophet Jeremiah wrote: "Thus saith the Lord of hosts, the God of Israel . . . I have made the earth, the man and the beast that are upon the ground, by My great power and by My outstretched arm" (Jer. 27: 4, 5).

The origin of life is one of the most debated topics of the day. I shall not attempt to enter into an academic discussion of the matter. The physicist is still grappling with it. We shall continue to confine our study in this chapter to the Word of God. The commandment under consideration was given by God, and that is the reason we give it solemn and serious thought. Therefore, whatever God has to say about life will be sufficient to guide us in this study.

However diversified the opinions of scientists and scholars may be, we have a clear and declarative statement as to the origin of human life—

"And the LORD God formed man of the dust of the ground, and breathed into his nostrils the breath of life; and man became a living soul" (Gen. 2: 7).

In the first chapter of Genesis the word "created" appears three times, and it describes that creative act of God by which He brought into existence the material universe (1:1), animal life (1:21), and *man* (1:27). Here the word translated "created" means "to bring into existence out of nothing." The prominent teaching is that neither the universe, animals, nor man is self-originated. Genesis is the book of beginnings, and its predominant purpose is to record the beginning of human life.

The origin of man was the crowning work in creation. Of such great consequence was this that the Holy Trinity, Father, Son, and Holy Spirit, counselled together, saying: "Let Us make man" (Gen. 1:26).... "So God created man" (1:27). Evolution declares "that life originated in a primordial germ, a protoplasmic cell, living, but structureless. From this microscopic beginning life developed by the principle of evolution along the lines of heredity, natural selection, adaptation to environment, and the struggle for existence, from lower to higher powers of life, from these to higher still, till ultimately it culminated in man." But the Scriptures deal the death-blow to the evolutionary theory. David said by the Holy Spirit: "I am fearfully and wonderfully made" (Ps. 139:14). To this testimony Elihu, the son of Barachel, adds: "The Spirit of God hath made me, and the breath of the Almighty hath given me life" (Job 33:4). Saint Paul testifies that it was our Lord who brought all things into being: "For by Him were all things created, that are in heaven, and that are in earth, visible and invisible, whether they be thrones, or dominions, or principalities, or powers: all things are created by Him and for Him" (Col. 1:16). The Apostle John said: "All things were made by Him; and without Him was not anything made that was made" (John 1:3).

Every inhabitant of Heaven and of earth is indebted to Him for its life.

Man is the possession of God by creative right Therefore we cannot place too high an estimate on human life. The Lord Jesus Himself sought to impress upon the Pharisees something of the sacredness of life when He said: "Have ye not read, that He which made them at the beginning made them male and female?" (Matt. 19: 4). The first man is the direct creation of God, and from Adam have sprung all the nations of the earth. "The God that made the world and all things therein, He, being Lord of heaven and earth . . . made of one every nation of men to dwell on all the face of the earth . . . for in Him we live, and move, and have our being; as certain even of your own poets have said, For we are also His offspring" (Acts 17: 24, 26, 28, R.V.). With positiveness and authority the Apostle states that the bounds of all human habitation are fixed by God. We all are the offspring of His workmanship. So when God lays down the sixth commandment, He is making no unfair demand. All He asks is that we do not destroy that which is rightfully His very own.

2. THE SUBSTANCE OF HUMAN LIFE.

Since human life was created by God, whatever the original creature consisted of was the result of God's thought. We know that the value of an item depends largely upon its content. We can see immediately that if God considers life of inestimable value, it is not only because He created it, but because of what life's substance is. David asked: "What is man, that Thou art mindful of him?" (Ps. 8: 4). This is a good question and calls for a careful investigation of the Scriptures. What

man is now and what man was before the fall call
for different answers if we look upon man in relation
to his likeness to the Godhead.   While it is true that
the image of God was marred in man because of the
fall, the component parts of man are virtually the same
as when he was created.   Even though man's likeness
to God has not been restored, and will not be until we
see Christ as He is (1 John 3:2), God still looks
upon man as His own creation, and therefore sets a
high appraisal upon his life.

When I was a boy there lived on our street a family
one of whom was a small girl who bore a close resemblance to her mother.   One day this child got hold of
some matches, and was striking them for her own
amusement when her clothing caught fire.   Severely
burned, she was rushed to a nearby hospital.   Through
immediate and careful treatment her life was spared,
but ugly scars marred her features.   One of the very
noticeable changes was the loss of mother-likeness. Yet,
I dare say that she got more attention, and greater
care was exercised in her favor than in that of the
rest of the family.   Though man no longer bears the
image and likeness of God, His love for man and His
regard for human life has not lessened in any degree.
The commandment, "Thou shalt not kill" is God's
safe-guard for human life.

"What is man?" asks David.   Made in the likeness
of God, man is a trinity.   He is spirit and soul and
body.   He exists in three corresponding parts.   The
Apostle Paul said: "I pray God your whole *spirit* and
soul and *body* be preserved blameless unto the coming
of our Lord Jesus Christ" (1 Thess. 5:23).   The
ability of man to know is furnished him by his spirit:

"For what man knoweth the things of a man, save the spirit of man which is in him" (1 Cor. 2: 11). Man also is a soul, and the soul is the seat of his emotional nature, his affections, his natural instincts. But man is also a body, and this body was formed "of the dust of the ground" (Gen. 2: 7). "The first man is of the *earth, earthly*" (1 Cor. 15: 47). The Scriptures distinguish between the visible and the invisible parts of man. When speaking of the bodily suffering that he endured Paul said: "For which cause we faint not; but though our *outward man* perish, yet the *inward man* is renewed day by day" (2 Cor. 4: 16). Jesus said: "Fear not them which kill the *body*, but are not able to kill the *soul*" (Matt. 10: 28).

Man is the offspring of both Heaven and earth, moulded, or fashioned, by the hand of God. His body is composed of the same elements of the dust upon which he treads; and his spirit is the very breath of God, the nature of the Creator Himself. Man, then, is God's masterpiece of creation. To God, human life is valuable, for He has made man in His own image. Human life is not now the same as when God brought it forth. It has been degraded and disfigured by sin. Nevertheless, "this commandment . . . flings a fiery law around the life of every human being, reserving to Him who first bestowed it the right to end it" (*Dr. G. Campbell Morgan*).

3. THE SAVING OF HUMAN LIFE.

Since God is the source and substance of life, He alone should have the right to decide when it should terminate. "Thou shalt not kill" is a commandment that finds application to all men. It is not confined to gangsters or professional gunmen. By a common carelessness men show that they do not value life, particularly when it is not their own. Hence the sixth commandment.

Of course, the commandment forbids wilful murder. There is no more fiendish crime than the deliberate act of taking another's life. It is cruel and criminal whether done directly and deliberately, as Cain slew Abel, or by proxy, as in the case of David when he murdered Uriah the Hittite. Many a murderer would have liked to rescind his deed, but it was too late. It was within his power to take a life, but he was powerless to restore that life. Some wrongs can be made right, but never the killing of human life. A man who does not regard the life of another is a menace to society. Many murders are born of sudden passion and enraged vengeance. Recently a prominent citizen of one of our large cities, upon finding his wife in the embrace of another man, suddenly slew his rival suitor. The rapidly growing number of murderers who are apprehended by law show what little value is placed upon human life. That which God regards as sacred is becoming more and more despised by men.

Not every person who has killed another can be charged with murder, for it is possible to kill and yet not to murder. I am thinking of the larger numbers who have died because of the sinful risk and carelessness of someone else. Recently two pilots flew a plane so low over an airfield crowded with spectators that a woman's head was completely severed from her body. They admitted that their "prank" was only meant to "throw a scare into the crowd." The death-toll resulting from speeding automobile drivers mounts up annually. Both men and women appear before our courts daily for reckless driving while under the influence of intoxicating liquors and beer. Someone has said that every drunken driver is a potential killer. It is a violation of the Law of God when we expose either ourselves or others to unnecessary risks. There have been many innocent children and adults whose lives have been prematurely snuffed-out by some thoughtless or drunken killer at the wheel of an automobile.

Then, too, this law forbids suicide. I speak tenderly. Doubtless there have been many who have taken their own lives while suffering from a form of insanity. But, as Dr. Boardman has said: "Let us not be too sentimental here: for even what is called "insanity" if oftentimes a moral madness rather than a mental —a species of mania for which the sufferer himself is to blame. And suicide, when committed by a sane person, is murder." It is wrong to fling away our own life, whether we do it suddenly, or slowly by degrees. The sane suicide is a murderer.

There are men and women who die a premature death because they indulge in harmful pleasures. It is proven beyond doubt or question that the use of tobacco has a decided ill-effect on the circulatory and respiratory system of the human body. It is a known fact in the field of medicine that smoking is a common cause of gastric ulcers. The highest medical authorities, including Johns Hopkins University and the Mayo Foundation, have concluded after clinical research, that the use of tobacco is one of the most important causes of coronary disease of the heart. Authoritative statistical findings show that smoking has decided effects on longevity. Nicotine deprives the person who inhales tobacco-smoke of an average of ten years of his life. To the smoker life is worth very little if it can be squandered so cheaply. We speak of this practice because it is a common one among church-goers as well as the non-churched. However, there are numerous other pleasures of this world that are having the same evil effects upon the human race.

Permit me to speak frankly of the shameful yet frequent sin of infanticide, the intentional killing of an infant child. Thousands of unwanted babies have been murdered before birth. Pre-natal infanticide is a growing practice among young married women as well as among the unmarried. Life is frequently snuffed-out before the little babe has felt a mother's caress or known her care. Our country is overrun with "quack doctors" who perform large numbers of illegal operations. The person who knows anything of what is going on in the world today knows that this crime has reduced the birth-rate to the danger-point of the destruction of the race. I do not choose to enter into a discussion of the problem of conjugality and posterity. See "What Does The Bible Teach About Birth Control?" by Keith L. Brooks. I am aware of the fact that innocence and decency have been brushed aside, and that a shameful and suggestive frankness has taken its place. However, it is sufficient to state here that it is nothing short of murder to destroy an unborn, unwanted baby. In this wholesale slaughter of the innocents, truly paganism is on the incline.

Coupled with the sixth commandment is the problem of war. I shall not now enter into a lengthy discussion of this problem though I have made a careful study of

the Christian and war. However, I find that I cannot
possibly endorse the teaching of pacifism. Human
governments are divine institutions (Rom. 13:1), and
every man is subject to the higher powers. On more
than one occasion God vindicated His righteousness by
sanctioning national warfare. The sixth commandment
cannot be interpreted "Thou shalt not kill" without
qualification. Such an interpretation would prohibit the
preparation of meat for food. Furthermore, it would
cast a reflection on God's perfect judgment when He
said. "Whoso sheddeth man's blood, by man shall his
blood be shed" (Gen. 9:6), and, "He that killeth man
shall surely be put to death" (Lev. 24:17). I find
that neither war nor capital punishment creates any
problem relative to the sixth commandment. See "Does
The Bible Sanction War?" by Harold Snider.

It is not enough that Christians refrain from doing
actual bodily harm to one another. The application
of this Commandment goes far deeper than the taking
of human life. Our Lord not only condemns the act
of killing: He forbids the passion that prompts the
act. Jesus said: "Ye have heard that it was said by
them of old time, Thou shalt not kill . . . But I say
unto you, That whosoever is angry with his brother
without a cause shall be in danger of the judgment"
(Matt. 5:21, 22). Here Christ is placing His approval
upon the Mosaic Law, but even more, He is expounding
and applying its truth more fully. Jesus' interpretation
of the Mosaic Law deals with the human heart before
any outward act of murder is committed, "For out of
the heart proceed evil thoughts, *murders*" (Matt. 15:
19). The passionate and petulant Christian who hates
his brother secretly is guilty of violating the Holy com-

mands of the Lord, for "Whosoever hateth his brother is a murderer" (1 John 3: 15). The Apostle Peter exhorted believers: "Let none of you suffer as a murderer" (1 Pet. 4: 15).

We may conclude that the Sixth Commandment is a call to exercise and express love toward each other. It is not given to the Christian to retaliate or to seek revenge. "Recompense to no man evil for evil . . . Dearly beloved, avenge not yourselves, but rather give place unto wrath: for it is written, Vengeance is Mine; I will repay, saith the Lord" (Rom. 12: 17, 19). When dealing with others as Christians, we must remember that "We do not war after the flesh: for the weapons of our warfare are not carnal" (2 Cor. 10: 3, 4). Let us follow in the steps of the Saviour "Who, when He was reviled, reviled not again; when He suffered, He threatened not" (1 Pet. 2: 23). Hatred is the root of all murder. Beloved, let us love one another.

THE SANCTITY OF THE BODY

THE SEVENTH COMMANDMENT

"Thou shalt not commit adultery" (Exod. 20: 14).

CHAPTER VIII

THE SANCTITY OF THE BODY

"Thou shalt not commit adultery" (Exod. 20: 14).

ONE of the miracles of the Scriptures is its applicability to every condition, thought, intent, and desire of mankind from the fall of the first human being to the last ones to live in an earthly habitation. One of the miracles of sin has been its unchangeableness in character through all the ages of its existence. Knowing "what is in man," God placed Himself on record in no uncertain terms as being opposed to adultery in the heart of any human being. Knowing that the natural heart will never evolve into any degree of perfection, He reiterated His stand against the loose morals of unmarried couples and the lack of fidelity of husband and wife. The flagrant violation of the Seventh Commandment calls for a frank discussion of a sin that has broken homes, wrecked lives, and sent great numbers to prison and to death. We are in full agreement with Dr. Morgan, when he said that there is no subject perhaps more difficult to deal with faithfully, and yet there is none demanding more honest and fearless handling.

1. THE DEFINITION OF THE SIN.

Adultery may be defined as sexual unfaithfulness or a violation of the marriage-bed. In Scripture any manner of lewdness, unchastity, idolatry, or apostasy was looked upon as adultery. An unchaste or an unholy alliance may be termed as adulterous, even though it does not involve sexual relations. God is represented in the Old Testament as the Husband of Israel, while Jesus Christ is spoken of in the New Testament as the Bridegroom of those whom He has redeemed. Therefore, any unfaithfulness to covenant vows or any thought or deed that does despite to the Christian ethic is adulterous.

Doubtless the thought connected with the Seventh Commandment is that of sexual unfaithfulness. Though it is one of the vilest, still it is one of the most prevalent sins of our age. Under the Mosaic Law it was considered a gross crime punishable by immediate death. "And the man that committeth adultery with another man's wife, even he that committeth adultery with his neighbor's wife, the adulterer and the adulteress shall surely be put to death" (Lev. 20: 10). When sexual intercourse is engaged in by the unmarried, it is called *fornication*. "But fornication . . . let it not once be named among you" (Eph. 5: 3). "Abstain from fornication" (1 Thess. 4: 3). "Whoremongers (or fornicators) . . . shall have their part in the lake which burneth with fire and brimstone: which is the second death" (Rev. 21: 8).

The prophet Hosea writes of Israel as being the adulterous wife of Jehovah. "Let her therefore put away her whoredoms out of her sight, and her adulteries from between her breasts" (Hos. 2: 2). We cannot interpret these words to mean merely a sexual unfaithfulness on the part of the children of Israel. The word *"adulteries"* here has to do with adulterous objects, and in Scripture that which is adulterous is idolatrous. When any person embraces an idolatrous or corrupt object, he is said to be adulterous. Through the prophet Jeremiah, the Lord said: "I have seen thine *adulteries*, and thy neighing, the lewdness of thy whoredom, and thine abominations on the hills in the fields. Woe unto thee, O Jerusalem! wilt thou not be made clean? when shall it once be?" (Jer. 13:27). Christ referred to this age as an "adulterous and sinful generation" (Mark 8:38). "The word *adulterous* is undoubtedly used in its broadest sense, and thus refers to the idolatry of the nation." *   Adultery and idolatry are expressed as synonymous terms in the Lord's message to Ezekiel—"With their idols have they committed adultery" (Ezek. 23:37); and also in the words of the risen Christ to the Apostle John when He condemned the doctrine of Balaam who taught Balac to cast a stumbling-block before the children of Israel, "to eat things sacrificed unto idols, and to commit fornication" (Rev. 2:14).

An unholy or worldly alliance is adulterous. The Apostle James said: "Ye adulterers and adulteresses, know ye not that the friendship of the world is enmity with God? Whosoever therefore will be a friend of the world is the enemy of God" (James 4:4). In one sense of the word we violate the Seventh Commandment when we choose worldly companions or engage in worldly pastime.

One last statement, uttered by the Lord Jesus, will serve in this definition of the sin of adultery. In His Sermon on the Mount Jesus said: "Ye have heard

---

* *Dr. E. Schuyler English.*

that it was said by them of old time, Thou shalt not commit adultery: but I say unto you, That whosoever looketh on a woman to lust after her hath committed adultery with her already in his heart" (Matt. 5: 27, 28). One may be guilty of the sin of adultery and never engage in the overt act. The sin that curses is a sin of the heart, "for out of the heart proceed . . . adulteries, fornications" (Matt. 15: 19). By our thoughts and imaginations we may break this Law of God.

2. THE DISTINCTION OF THE SEXES.

The glorious climax of the creative week was God's masterpiece, Adam and Eve. Amidst the beauties of Eden, Adam stands complete, the crown and culmination of God's creation. He is a man—the male sex. "And the Lord God formed man of the dust of the ground, and breathed into his nostrils the breath of life; and man became a living soul" (Gen. 2: 7). But God had not finished His work of creation. He discovered in Adam a disquietude and an indefinable want: and the Lord God said, It is not good that the man should be alone; I will make him an help meet for him" (Gen. 2: 18). And then we have the record of God's method of the creation of the woman—

"And the Lord God caused a deep sleep to fall upon Adam, and he slept: and he took one of his ribs, and closed up the flesh instead thereof; and the rib, which the Lord God had taken from man, made He a woman, and brought her unto the man. And Adam said, This is now bone of my bones, and flesh of my flesh: she shall be called Woman, because she was taken out of Man"

(Gen. 2: 21-23).

We see in Adam's words, "Bone of my bones, and flesh of my flesh," an essential unity of the man and the woman. There was a likeness and a similarity between them, for the woman was taken out of the side of the man.

Nevertheless there is a dissimilarity between them that even their resemblance cannot conceal. There are graces and delicacies in womanhood that never were given to man. And there are virtues and excellencies in man that never were assigned to woman. The Bible teaches plainly that man and woman are different. A woman is not like a man, nor is a man like a woman. So different are they, the one from the other, that God designed their garments to be different. "The woman shall not wear that which pertaineth unto a man, neither shall a man put on a woman's garment: for all that do so are abomination unto the LORD thy God" (Deut. 22: 5). God is opposed to women's appearing masculine. How grieved He must be as He beholds the trend of this age! Woman today is seeking to unsex herself and to be like man. "It is only as woman remains womanly, that woman remains imperial," says Dr. Boardman.

God has intended also that man remain masculine. Therefore it is sinful for a man to appear effeminate. The Holy Spirit catalogues the effeminate with adulterers, thieves, and drunkards: "Be not deceived: neither fornicators, nor idolaters, nor adulterers, *nor effeminate,* nor abusers of themselves with mankind, nor thieves, nor covetous, nor drunkards, nor revilers, nor extortioners, shall inherit the kingdom of God" (1 Cor. 6: 9, 10). When a man becomes weak and womanish he loses the strength of character and manliness that God intended he should possess.

The man and woman as God created them made the first and the ideal bridal. Marriage is a divine institution dating back before the fall of man. The man was not complete without the woman, nor the woman without the man. Here the human race differs from the angels. Of all the human relations there is none so sacred and personal as marriage, "Therefore shall a man leave his father and his mother, and shall cleave unto his wife: and they shall be one flesh" (Gen. 2: 24). The man and the woman being organically joined by God, none but God can separate. It is a union for life, "till death us do part."

"What therefore God hath joined together, let not man put asunder" (Mark 10: 9).

3. THE DESTRUCTION OF MARRIAGE SACREDNESS.

"Thou shalt not commit adultery" is God's command given to protect the sacredness of marriage. The marriage-book speaks of marriage as the "holy estate of matrimony instituted of God, adorned and beautified by the presence of Christ, and is commended of Saint Paul to be honorable among all men; and therefore is not by any to be entered into unadvisedly, but reverently, discretely, and in the fear of God." Great numbers have stood at the marriage altar listening to God's views on this divine institution, only to desecrate it in after-years.

When God gave Adam his wife there was but one man and one woman. This was the Lord's ideal of a perfect marriage, one wife for one husband, and no more. The blessedness of the years to follow, the harmony in the home, and the future of society, depended upon man's view of this indissoluble union. Until sin entered the lives of Adam and Eve the idea of separation had not been born. Their sin was a violation of a law of God making it comparatively easy for man to break other of God's commandments. Hence the subsequent violation of the marriage law.

The privileges of the sexes in marriage were never to be indulged in by other than legally married couples. To do so would defile the marriage-bed. It is this prohibition that we have in the Seventh Commandment. Yet fornication and adultery are common today. There is lewdness and lechery among young and old alike. Venereal diseases are widespread over our land. Decency and morality are so ignored that the rate of illegitimate births steadily increases. Reports from the Surgeon General's Office of the United States Army tell us that although no men with venereal diseases were accepted into the armed forces, yet among the new men who were drafted there are large numbers who have become so badly infected that the army has a high percent of the deadly syphilis and gonorrhea. In view of such a flagrant transgression of this sacred Law, America can expect God to smite in judgment. Both married and single are guilty, and this paints a dark future for the American way of life. With the future generation being raised in the midst of such debauchery and degeneracy we look for a fearful chastising.

The plurality of mates in marriage is a violation of the Seventh Commandment. The Pharisees came to Jesus about the matter of divorce in an endeavor to tempt Him and to entangle Him in His speech. They asked:

"Is it lawful for a man to put away his wife for every cause? And He answered and said unto them, Have ye not read, that He which made them at the beginning made them male and female, and said, For this cause shall a man leave father and mother, and shall cleave to his wife: and they twain shall be one flesh? Wherefore they are no more twain, but one flesh. What therefore God hath joined together, let not man put asunder. They say unto Him, Why did Moses then command to give a writing of divorcement, and to put her away? He saith unto them, Moses because of the hardness of your hearts suffered you to put away your wives: but from the beginning it was not so"

(Matt. 19: 3-8).

In His reply our Lord taught clearly that from the beginning of the creation of man it was God's purpose that no earthly power nor man-made ordinance should sever that which God had joined together. In spite of the fact that sin caused the fall of man, God did not change in the matter. However, He did make one provision whereby a man or a woman may be divorced from his or her adulterous mate. Let it be understood that God never endorsed nor approved divorce. Christ said plainly to the Pharisees that Moses "suffered" (or allowed) them to put away their wives. Because of sin, God sometimes allows things that He would not permit were the sin never committed. The death of Christ is an example of this. Man, by his transgression, fell and was severed from the fellowship of God. In love and mercy God suffered (or allowed) his Son Jesus Christ to die on the cross in order that sinners could be reconciled to Him. Sexual unfaithfulness on the part of a husband or a wife is the only ground for divorce. In mercy God suffers this for the benefit of the innocent person. Jesus said:

"It hath been said, Whosoever shall put away his wife, let him give her a writing of divorcement: but I say unto you, That whosoever shall put away his wife, saving for the cause of fornication, causeth her to commit adultery: and whosoever shall marry her that is divorced committeth adultery" (Matt. 5: 31, 32).

"He saith unto them, Moses because of the hardness of your hearts suffered you to put away your wives: but from the beginning it was not so. And I say unto you, Whosoever shall put away his wife, except it be for fornication, and shall marry another, committeth adultery: and whoso marrieth her which is put away doth commit adultery" (Matt. 19: 8, 9).

Remember, dear reader, "From the beginning it was not so," but when man destroyed the sacredness of the marriage relationship, divorce was made permissible by God. Though the ordinances and laws of man provide for divorce on other grounds, it is never recognized by God except where one is guilty of adultery. Furthermore, *it is Christ's plain teaching that no divorced person may re-marry.* *

"And he saith unto them, Whosoever shall put away his wife, and marry another, committeth adultery against her" (Mark 10: 11).

"And if a woman shall put away her husband, and be married to another, she committeth adultery"
                                                    (Mark 10: 12).
The Apostle Paul adds:

"Know ye not, brethren (for I speak to them that know the law), how the law hath dominion over a man as long as he liveth?" (Rom. 7: 1).

---

* A more thorough study on the subject of Marriage and Divorce is taken up by the author in another series of messages.

"For the woman which hath an husband is bound by the law to her husband so long as he liveth; but if the husband be dead, she is loosed from the law of her husband" (Rom. 7: 2).

"So then if, while her husband liveth, she be married to another man, she shall be called an adulteress: but if her husband be dead, she is free from that law; so that she is no adulteress, though she be married to another man" (Rom. 7: 3).

In the language of Christ and the Apostles we have the divine commentary on the Seventh Commandment. When we are following the teaching of the New Testament exposition we are obeying God, and we may expect His blessing upon our lives.

In His teaching on adultery our Lord went deeper into the subject than what is involved in the sexual act. Jesus said: "Ye have heard that it was said by them of old time, Thou shalt not commit adultery:

"But I say unto you, That whosoever looketh on a woman to lust after her hath committed adultery with her already in his heart" (Matt. 5: 27, 28).

"For from within, out of the heart of man, proceed evil thoughts, adulteries, fornications" (Mark 7: 21).

The crux of the matter then is not the sin and not the appetite; it is whether the heart is right with God. The sin that damns and destroys is a sin of the heart. When we have Christ within and have surrendered our will to Him, we will not engage in the indecencies of life.

"For ye are bought with a price: therefore glorify God in your body, and in your spirit, which are God's" (1 Cor. 6: 20).

CHAPTER IX
THE SIN OF STEALING

THE EIGHTH COMMANDMENT

"Thou shalt not steal" (Exod. 20: 15).

CHAPTER IX

THE SIN OF STEALING

"Thou shalt not steal" (Exod. 20: 15).

ARE you a thief? Many persons and surely most Christians pass over the injunction, "Thou shalt not steal," with a feeling of contentment that here is one commandment that they do not break. But let us weigh carefully the question, "Am I a robber?"

Stealing is one of the most common sins in the world today, for there is a tendency on the part of man to proceed in a clandestine manner to take by stealth that which is not his own. The desire to possess or to use for his own advantage has led man to purloin the rights and the property of his fellow-man. Martin Luther once said: "If all thieves—who nevertheless do not wish to be considered such—were to be hanged to the gallows, the world would soon be desolate, and would be without both executioners and gallows." God has given man certain rights in the world. But because we have impinged upon our neighbors' rights and so that we might respect the rights of each other, the eighth commandment was given.

1. How Are We Violators?

What is stealing? It may be the common pilfering of material values that places one in wrong relation with the law. One may be led to such stealing by poverty, laziness, drunkenness, or mental derangement. The number and degree of arrests for stealing increase annually, and it is all the more grievous in view of the fact that the average age of the thief becomes lower each year. Just this week our community grieved over the apprehension by law of three local eleven-year-old boys who had been breaking into business concerns and stealing large sums of money.

Most of us look upon such acts of stealing as wickedness, yet there are numerous methods of thieving which are glossed over and referred to in terminology that makes the guilty one appear innocent. In business it is often referred to as "the practice of the trade." There are business methods that are ostensibly legal, and business concerns who, by their chicaneries, swindle the rights of others to a fair value. The world has never been rid of the rogue of whom Amos spoke:

"Falsifying the balances by deceit," and those who "buy the poor for silver, and the needy for a pair of shoes; yea, and sell the refuse of the wheat"
(Amos 8: 5, 6).

After the Ten Commandments were given, the Mosaic System warned against such unfair dealings.

"Ye shall do no unrighteousness in judgment, in mete-yard, in weight, or in measure. Just balances, just weights, a just ephah, and a just hin, shall ye have: I am the LORD your God, which brought you out of the land of Egypt" (Lev. 19: 35, 36).

"Thou shalt not have in thy bag divers weights, a great and a small. Thou shalt not have in thine house divers measures, a great and a small. But thou shalt

THE SIN OF STEALING

**have a perfect and just weight, a perfect and just meas-
ure shalt thou have: that thy days may be lengthened in
the land which the LORD thy God giveth thee.   For
all that do such things, and all that do unrighteously, are
an abomination unto the LORD thy God"**

(Deut. 25: 13-16).

Many church-going, decent, respectable citizens became thieves when they filed their income-tax returns.
The government agent in our local office said that the
church is one of the wealthiest organizations in town,
or else its members are a lot of liars. How embarrass-
ing for some Christians in the day of reckoning when
they must give account of every such false report.
When the chief priests and scribes sent spies to our
Lord, they asked Him: "Is it lawful for us to give
tribute unto Caesar, or no?"   In His reply our Lord
said. "Show Me a penny.   Whose image and super-
scription hath it?   They answered and said, Caesar's.
And He said unto them, Render therefore unto Caesar
the things which be Caesar's, and unto God the things
which be God's" (Luke 20: 22-25).   The question
asked of Jesus was a political one, and it was pro-
pounded for the purpose of ensnaring Him into taking
a political stand.   But instead, He taught them that
man is indebted to the State whose coinage he uses in
trade.   This principle finds application to all men
everywhere.   If we fail to give an accurate assessment
of personal property, we are guilty of the sin of stealing.

Many people are known to scheme ways of beating
customs and dues on certain goods.   This is stealing.
The Apostle Paul said: "Render therefore to all their
dues: tribute to whom tribute is due; custom to whom

custom" (Rom. 13:7). Sometimes we are tempted to avoid rendering that which is due. The first time I made the trip from the United States to Canada by train I recall how resentful I felt of the Customs officer's examination of my personal effects. And yet how true that Christians should be the first to render dues to those in authority over us! Let the worldling, the child of Satan, plan his wiles to cheat and fraud. It is time for God's children to awake and arise to the need for purity, and leave the cheap, sordid tricks to the Devil's crowd.

We steal when we use the rights of another for our own profit. Some years ago I was employed by a large retail concern which issued a discount card to all employees. This card entitled the employee to a ten per cent reduction on the purchase of all merchandise. It was painful to see Christians who were employed elsewhere making large purchases of furniture, jewelry, and other commodities, and presenting the discount card of a friend in order to benefit themselves. This act was false and deceitful, for it necessitated forging the name of the person who was the rightful owner of the privilege.

One illustration from the Bible exposes such dealings. One of the most cunning and crafty characters in the Old Testament is Jacob. One day his brother Esau returned from the fields tired and hungry. Jacob had been preparing the family meal. When the odor of the pottage came to Esau's nostrils, he said to Jacob: "Feed me, I pray thee, with that same red pottage; for I am faint."

"And Jacob said, *Sell* me this day thy birthright" (Gen. 25:29-31).

Faint from hunger, Esau sold his birthright to his brother. Now when the Bible refers to Esau and this transaction, it states that he *sold* his birthright (Heb. 12: 16). We are not excusing nor exonerating Esau for his part in the deal, for we despise his actions. He did not value his God-given rights and in so doing despised their Giver. Yet it is strange that Jacob never is looked upon as having purchased the birthright from his brother. He is charged with having stolen it. By the same cunning, he afterward acquired the blessing from his aged father that was intended for Esau. How sad that this ancient patriarch and leader in Israel must be charged with the sin of stealing! Sadder still is the fact that Christians, after nineteen hundred years of gospel preaching, still employ the methods of Jacob.

We are no less guilty of violating this commandment when we steal another's reputation so as to limit his progress or his usefulness in this life. This is a common occurrence among those of the household of faith, and it usually arises out of a jealous spirit. Some Christians who are not very successful in helping themselves are sometimes quick to hurt others. This kind of stealing is devilish and damaging. It has always been a mystery to the writer why there are so few believers who can sincerely rejoice in another's success. We need to exercise the greatest of care in our speech so as not to cast aspersions upon the character and ability of others. Sometimes a depreciative look when the name of some brother is mentioned has caused others who were present to question the person named. Brethren, these things ought not to be.

Then, too, we must answer the charge of stealing time. Of this not a few of us are guilty. Man feels that he is master of his own time, and therefore is free to dispose of it at his own pleasure. But such is not the case. Each of us lives on borrowed time, and in God's time we shall have breathed our last breath and passed into a life "where they count not time by years." The Psalmist cried: "Remember how short my *time* is . . . What man is he that liveth, and shall not see death?" (Ps. 89: 47,48). Job asked: "Is there not an appointed *time* to man upon earth? Are not his days also like the days of an hireling?" (Job. 7: 1). If you are still in your sins, without Christ, God is saying: "Behold, now is the accepted *time;* behold, now is the day of salvation" (2 Cor. 6: 2). The thief of time who dies in his sins has robbed himself of everlasting life and Heaven.

We sometimes hear Christians speak of "killing time." To "kill time" means to give one's self to unimportant things for the purpose of preventing ennui, or weariness. The soul that seeks pleasure and pastime merely because there is nothing to do needs to pray that God will kindle the fire of revival within him. Similarly we speak of "losing time." It means to delay to take advantage of an opportunity. Or it may mean to move too slowly, as a watch or a clock would lose time. Those who kill or lose time are far removed from obeying the exhortation of God's Word, where we read: "Redeeming the time, because the days are evil" (Eph. 5: 16). The Apostle used this expression again when he wrote: "Walk in wisdom toward them that are without, *redeeming the time*" (Col. 4: 5). In each instance we have the thought of "buying up the opportunities." When the department stores run bargain sales, crowds gather to make purchases at a saving, customers deeming it wise to buy bargains at a reduced rate. Housewives lay aside everything and rush enthusiastically to buy up a commodity at a bargain-counter. So ought Christians to seize hold of every God-given opportunity to bring salvation and blessing to those who are in need. Now is the time to engage in serving our Blessed Lord. This is the appropriate and opportune time, for "To every thing there is a season, and a *time* to every purpose under the heaven" (Eccl. 3: 1). Let us follow in the steps of our Lord, who said: "I must work the works of Him that sent Me, while it is day: the night cometh, when no man can work" (John 9: 4).

Stealing is not always aggressive and active. It has been said that we can steal by simply doing nothing. The man who refuses to pay his debts is a thief. Some persons will buy or borrow without money, in good faith; but they never get to paying it back when they are able. Now it is no sin to borrow. Jesus borrowed a boat, a penny, and a colt. When Elisha increased the widow's oil, he said: "Go, borrow thee vessels abroad of all thy neighbors, even empty vessels; borrow not a few." Then when he filled the vessels with oil, he added: "Go, sell the oil, and pay thy debt" (2 Kings 4: 3-7).

Dr. G. Campbell Morgan offers a timely comment on this thought:

"It would be interesting, but extremely painful, to pass through the homes of thousands of church-members, instituting a rigid examination as to the ownership of all the books to be found therein. The habit of borrowing books is in itself pernicious, but the appalling extent of the carelessness as to the return of the same is hardly realized, because people forget that to borrow a book and not to return it is a theft. If these sentences should cause the discovery of some of my books, and they are returned to me, I shall be ever grateful for having had this opportunity of enforcing the eighth commandment."

The prophet Malachi records a fearful charge made by God to Israel when the Lord said: "Ye have robbed Me" (Mal. 3:8). The people said: "Wherein have we robbed Thee?" And God answers: "In tithes and offerings." Since it is a sin to fail to respect the rights and property of our fellow-men, how much greater is the sin of failing to respect the rights of Almighty God. The Christian steals when he refuses to give regularly and proportionately to the work of the Lord. I feel certain that not one of us would want to be charged with the sin of stealing; yet not a few of us have withheld from our Heavenly Father that which rightfully belongs to Him.

2. HOW ARE WE VICTORS?

Reckoning without God, men fail to recognize the Creator and Sustainer of all life and assume to themselves credit for that which God has in mercy provided. This was illustrated to the writer while he was distributing New Testaments to workers in the factories of Bristol. All but one man gladly received with expectancy the Scripture offered him. As the writer stood beside one man's machine and began to state the purpose of his visit, the worker, curtly interrupting and pointing to the Testament, arrogantly boasted: "That never put any food on my table. I worked for everything I ever got." One could not but remind him that if it were not for the mercy and grace of God, he might be unable to earn his living because of physical or mental incapacity.

God has said: "The silver is Mine, and the gold is Mine" (Haggai 2: 8). The Apostle Paul testifies, "For the earth is the Lord's, and the fulness thereof" (1 Cor. 10: 28). How foolish man is to live independently of God! "For we brought nothing into this world, and it is certain we can carry nothing out" (1 Tim. 6: 7). We would do well to consider our obligations to Him who has given us life.

True conversion makes a man honest. When Zacchæus was converted he had had a dark past. He was a hated publican upon whom the Jews had poured their hostility. But when Jesus saved him, he confessed his sins and made to the Lord a promise: "Behold, Lord, the half of my goods I give to the poor; and if I have taken any thing from any man by false accusation, I restore him fourfold" (Luke 19: 8). The genuineness and thoroughness of Zacchæus' conversion was indicated by his willingness to restore all the money he had unjustly taken from his fellow-citizens. It is a fact that when we are right with God we get right with man.

We can be led to victory over this sin when we see the ill and injury that it works to others. Greed, lust, and selfishness will blind us to the injury we cause others. Sometimes in our desire to get we lose sight of what it has cost the one from whom we have obtained. Whether we steal a man's money, his rights, or his good name we injure him; and sometimes the injury is a permanent one. David stole Uriah's wife, and the injury was irreparable. Everyone involved felt the blight and curse of David's sin. If he might have been forewarned of the forthcoming damage, I feel sure that David would have thought twice before stealing Bathsheba away from her husband. When Jacob stole the birthright and the blessing from Esau, Esau never fully recovered from the shock.

We may be led to victory over this sin by giving careful thought to the hardship that stealing works in the life of him who steals. There is the divine law of adjustment that reads: "Be not deceived; God is not mocked: for whatsoever a man soweth, that shall he also reap" (Gal. 6: 7). The Bible shows this law in operation in both the old and the New Testaments, both before and after the time of Christ upon earth. When David was king over Israel, Absalom his son sought to overthrow the kingdom and ascend to the throne by illegitimate means. We are told: "So Absalom stole the hearts of the men of Israel" (2 Sam. 15: 6, 7). But when he attempted to carry out his plot Absalom died a horrible death in the wilderness, and his body was cast into a great pit (2 Sam. 18: 9-17). If he had only known the consequences that awaited him, there is the possibility that he might never have attempted to steal the kingdom from his father.

The New Testament records a clear case against Ananias and Sapphira. We are told that they "sold a possession, and kept back part of the price" (Acts 5: 1, 2). But it was a sad and shameful end for the man and his wife. Before an opportunity was given them to enjoy the money, God struck them dead. Again it is reasonable to assume that Ananias and Sapphira would never have robbed God if they had known the price that they would have to pay for their sin. Not one of us can steal and escape retribution. If no one else has discovered your sin, be sure your sin will find you out.

In closing this meditation let me say that whatever your past may be, God stands ready to forgive all. "If we confess our sins, He is faithful and just to forgive us our sins, and to cleanse us from all unrighteousness" (1 John 1: 9). If you have been guilty, come now to the Saviour, and, having confessed all, make restitution wherever possible to those whom you have wronged. Then heed the admonition of the Apostle Paul, when he said:

"Let him that stole steal no more" (Eph. 4: 28).

THE STIGMA OF A FALSE WITNESS

THE NINTH COMMANDMENT

"Thou shalt not bear false witness against thy neighbor" (Exod. 20: 16).

CHAPTER X

THE STIGMA OF A FALSE WITNESS

"Thou shalt not bear false witness against thy neighbor"
(Exod. 20: 16).

LANGUAGE, the faculty of speech, is one of the most useful and necessary gifts ever bestowed by God upon mortals. It is by means of conveying their thoughts in words that men can understand and fellowship with one another. Almost all that we know has been brought to us through the medium of language. We depend largely upon what we have heard or read. In spite of the skepticism of man it is amazing how we trust and depend upon others.

But how sad when we use the gift of language to smear the reputation of another! The tongue is a difficult member to tame, and it has been the instrument of much slander, perjury, and salacious talk. The Apostle James has said: "The tongue is a fire, a world of iniquity: so is the tongue among our members, that it defileth the whole body, and setteth on fire the course of nature, and it is set on fire of hell" (James 3: 6). The poison-tongued talebearer is one of the world's worst offenders, for words are immortal and their damage far-reaching.

1. THE EXPLANATION OF FALSE WITNESS.

What is meant by bearing false witness? The command, "Thou shalt not bear false witness," demands that we be truthful. We have stated earlier in this volume that the third and the ninth commandments are closely related in that both deal with the sins of the tongue. In the third commandment we are forbidden to take the name of the Lord in vain. There God seeks to protect His own Name. But here in the ninth commandment we find God protecting our name by forbidding us to bear false witness against each other.

This commandment is frequently violated in the courts of law. Many men have been condemned because of a false testimony that someone gave against them. The primary purpose of our law courts is to guarantee justice among men. God charged the judges in Israel, saying: "Hear the causes between your brethren, and judge righteously between every man and his brother, and the stranger that is with him. Ye shall not respect persons in judgment but ye shall hear the small as well as the great" (Deut. 1: 16, 17). The offence of perjury is a misdemeanor that is pursued with scathing denunciation. The legalists of our Lord's Day bore false witness against Him when He stood on trial. How terrible will be the day of judgment for all who accused Christ! The person who takes an oath to tell the truth and then lies, must answer to God for violating the ninth commandment. A lie is wicked, but perjury is worse.

The ninth commandment forbids all kind of slander. It is criminal to utter maliciously a false tale or report about another in order to injure his reputation. When we vilify the good name of someone else we are allying ourselves with Satan himself who is the prince of slanderers. Slander is devilish, for the Devil is the accuser of the brethren (Rev. 12: 10).

Slander does not always show itself in a bold assertion. A most subtle form of slander can be insinuated in so small a thing as a question. When God praised Job by calling him "a perfect and an upright man, one that feareth God, and escheweth evil," Satan answered the Lord, and said: "Doth Job fear God for naught?" (Job 1: 8, 9). Notice that Satan does not make a positive charge against Job. He does not accuse Job of being a thief or an adulterer. Satan used the sly and shrewd question method. You see he did not speak out against Job, he merely asked a question. How utterly devilish! Behind that question there was the hellish system of slander. This common method of bearing false witness is too frequently practised among Christians. "Is the Rev.——— true to the Word?" "Would——— qualify for such a position?" "Is ——— an honest man?" These and similar questions, when asked maliciously, bear false witness. Though they incur no danger of a charge against the one asking the question, I feel sure that such Satanic methods will never escape the eye and the righteous judgment of God.

But a man's reputation can be easily ruined by a lie whispered in secret, as by perjury in a courtroom or by an open, slanderous attack. The Bible speaks out against whisperers and backbiters, both of whom are guilty before God.

"Being filled with all unrighteousness, fornication, wickedness, covetousness, maliciousness; full of envy, murder, debate, deceit, malignity; whisperers, backbiters, haters of God, despiteful, proud, boasters, inventors of evil things, disobedient to parents" (Rom. 1: 29, 30).

"For I fear, lest, when I come, I shall not find you such as I would, and that I shall be found unto you such

as ye would not: lest there be debates, envyings, wraths, strifes, backbitings, whisperings, swellings, tumults"
                                    (2 Cor. 12: 20).

A whisperer is a secret slanderer who peddles secret reports. His words have in them the sting of an adder. Dr. William R. Newell tells of a modest, respectable young woman who was secretly slandered by a jealous rival. Being unable to overcome the malicious scandal that was a falsehood, she died in less than one year. God alone has the records of that vast host of unfortunate victims who have been driven to their graves prematurely because of someone's evil tongue. David testified: "Mine enemies speak evil of me . . . all that hate me whisper together against me" (Ps. 41: 5, 7).

There are those too who, by tale-bearing, spread slanderous reports. People should never disclose the unlovely things they have heard about others. The information may not always be true or accurate. And even if it is true, love covers a multitude of sins; it never spreads them about. "Thou shalt not go up and down as a talebearer among thy people" (Lev. 19: 16). There is a proverb that warns us against such practices —"He that covereth a transgression seeketh love; but he that repeateth a matter separateth very friends" (Prov. 17: 9). Christians ought to exercise great care so as not to hear or speak unkind things about others. The Apostle Paul speaks of those that "learn to be idle, wandering about from house to house; and not only idle, but tattlers also and busybodies, speaking things which they ought not" (1 Tim. 5: 13).

Another way of bearing false witness is by the common practice of lying, even thought it does injury to no one but ourselves. To begin with, lying is one of the things that God hates. "These six things doth the Lord hate: yea, seven are an abomination unto Him: a proud look, a lying tongue . . . a false witness that speaketh lies, and he that soweth discord among brethren" (Prov. 6: 16-19). Lying is satanic, for the Devil is the father of lies. "When he speaketh a lie, he speaketh of his own: for he is a liar, and the father of it" (John 8: 44). Liars belong to the Devil's family, and would do wisely to change over to God's family by being born again. Whenever a man lies he is led of Satan to do so. When Ananias kept back part of his money and pretended that he had given all, Peter said: "Ananias, why hath Satan filled thine heart to lie to the Holy Ghost, and to keep back part of the price of the land?" (Acts 5: 3).

Even among believers this sin is not uncommon. The Apostle Paul found it needful to exhort Christians, "Lie not one to another, seeing that ye have put off the old man with his deeds" (Col. 3: 9). Let us not forget that "all liars shall have their part in the lake which burneth with fire and brimstone: which is the second death" (Rev. 21: 8). Those of us who have named the Name of Christ need to pray as did the Psalmist: "Remove from me the way of lying" (Ps. 119: 29), and as Solomon: "Remove far from me vanity and lies" (Prov. 30: 8). God is the sovereign, unerring Lie Detector. He has said: "The lip of truth shall be established forever: but a lying tongue is but for a moment" (Prov. 12: 19).

We can bear false witness also by giving false flattery. I am not stating that we should not honestly compliment where this is due. I feel that Dr. Chappell spoke the truth when he said that the machinery of this world would run far more smoothly if it were more frequently oiled by the fine lubricant of appreciation. It is true that we fail too often to express our gratitude. On the other hand, there is far too much flattery among Christians. Elihu cautioned against it when he said: "Let me not, I pray you, accept any man's person, neither let me give flattering titles unto man. For I know not to give flattering titles, in so doing my Maker would soon take me away" (Job 32: 21, 22). The true servant of the Lord will not apply such methods to gain the favor of others. The Apostle Paul testified: "For neither at any time used we flattering words" (1 Thess. 2: 5). The Scriptures make it plain that flattery is a worldly method of getting ahead. It was predicted of Antiochus Epiphanes, the "little horn" of Daniel, chapter eleven, that he would "obtain the kingdom by flatteries" (Dan. 11: 21). The Christian should avoid this practice as well as those who are given to the habitual flattery of others. "Meddle not with him that flattereth with his lips" (Prov. 20: 19).

But the violation of the Ninth Commandment is not always active. It is sometimes passive. We can bear false witness by our silence as strongly as by our speech. The Lord convicted the writer of this not very long ago. A group of laymen and preachers had gathered at a luncheon for the purpose of discussing plans relative to launching an evangelistic campaign. During the course of conversation a loose-tongued brother spoke disreputably about a brother-minister. I was sufficiently well acquainted with the man about whom the story was told, to know that it was not true. Yet I remained silent, and by so doing felt that I had shared in bearing the false witness.

2. THE EFFECTS OF A FALSE WITNESS.

Words are immortal. They do not die with the death of the one who utters them. Jesus said: "But I say unto you, That every idle word that men shall speak, they shall give account thereof in the day of judgment" (Matt. 12: 36). This means that all who bear false witness will reap the fruit of that sin. "For by thy words thou shalt be justified, and by thy words thou shalt be condemned" (Matt. 12: 37). The judgment-seat of Christ will bring shame and disappointment to many Christians who have practised speaking disparagingly of other brethren. The Apostle James has said: "If any man among you seem to be religious, and bridleth not his tongue, but deceiveth his own heart, this man's religion is vain" (James 1: 26). The Word of the Lord warns: "Whoso privily slandereth his neighbor, him will I cut off" (Ps. 101: 5). It is quite clear that the person who is guilty of this damaging sin will reap the effects to his own hurt.

If the guilty one alone felt the evil effects of his sin, that would not be so bad in itself. But the person against whom we speak is oftentimes the innocent sufferer. Whenever we violate this command we rob of his reputation the one against whom we have witnessed. We can see how obedience to the command acts as a safeguard for a man's name. Each of us values his reputation. We are concerned about what others think of us. It might be well to bear in mind that reputation and character are two widely different things. Holland said: "Character lives in a man, reputation outside of him." Character is what a man actually is, reputation is what others suppose him to be. No one can injure our character by what might be said against us, and, after all, character is by far the more important of the two. But one's reputation can be ruined by the evil-speaking of another. It is such injurious talk that is here forbidden.

The stigma of a false witness affects society at large. It has been the divider of friendships of many years' standing. "A whisperer separateth chief friends" (Prov. 16: 28). "He that repeateth a matter separateth very friends" (Prov. 17: 9). We live in a world that has never known freedom from strife and war. How careful we should be so as not to cause more strife! Let us remember that "The words of a talebearer are as wounds" (Prov. 18: 8), and very often the wound is never healed. But, "Where there is no talebearer, the strife ceaseth" (Prov. 26: 20). When we have ceased from this devilish practice we have made a valuable contribution to society.

It was a false witness against God that plunged the whole human race into sin and judgment. God's words to Adam and Eve were unmistakably clear when He said: "Of the tree of the knowledge of good and evil, thou shalt not eat of it: for in the day that thou eatest thereof *thou shalt surely die*" (Gen. 2: 17). Afterward Satan came upon the scene bearing false witness against the Lord when he said to the woman: "*Ye shall not surely die*" (Gen. 3: 4). Because of one man's disobedience instigated by a lie, all were made sinners, and many have gone into eternal condemnation.

Think of the influence of the false witness borne by some who occupy pulpits! Because these men behind the sacred desk have questioned, criticized, and even denied the Bible as the Inspired Word of God, the faith of multitudes of our young people has been shaken. This apostasy is the forerunner of the moral declension and crime wave that are sweeping our nation today. The world is in desperate straits, and nothing will help the situation like the straightforward proclamation of the Word of God as it embraces all of the eternal Verities of the faith. Ministers need to heed the charge and challenge of the Apostle Paul when he wrote to Timothy: "I charge thee therefore before God, and the Lord Jesus Christ, who shall judge the quick and the dead at His appearing and His kingdom; preach the Word; be instant in season, out of season; reprove, rebuke, exhort, with all longsuffering and doctrine" (2 Tim. 4: 1, 2). The pernicious doctrines of the modernist and cult leaders are sending multitudes to eternal doom, but how solemn will be the day of reckoning for these bearers of a false witness!

None but those in Satan's power will continue to lie, exaggerate, lead astray, slander, or cast aspersions. Maybe you have been guilty of that very thing which is here forbidden. If this is so, come to God in prayer, and confess your sin to Him. And wherever possible, seek to set those persons straight who have been misguided by your false witness. God will forgive you, and you will find that your Christian brother or sister will receive you warmly. We should have the high aspiration and a burning passion to be known for the truth. May it be testified of us even as it was of one of old,

"Demetrius hath good report of all men, and of the truth itself" (3 John 12).

CHAPTER XI
THE SELFISH LIFE DENOUNCED

THE TENTH COMMANDMENT

"Thou shalt not covet" (Exod. 20: 17).

CHAPTER XI

THE SELFISH LIFE DENOUNCED

"Thou shalt not covet" (Exod. 20: 17).

THE tenth word of the Decalogue differs noticeably from those which precede it in that it deals with the inner recesses of the heart. It is possible to violate this commandment and never be exposed to our fellow-men. Covetousness may never break out in an overt act. However, we cannot judge another man's desires or his thoughts: God alone must do that. The Tenth Commandment does not deal much with overt acts, but it regulates the heart. Inasmuch as "Thou, Lord, knowest the hearts of all men" (Acts 1: 24), we ought to pay earnest heed to what this commandment teaches.

1. THE COMMAND.

Since the Law says plainly: "Thou shalt not covet," why should it be surprising to some Christians to learn that coveting is sinful? To violate what is forbidden in this commandment is to sin against God. Jesus said: "For from within, out of the heart of men, proceed evil thoughts, adulteries, fornications, murders, thefts, *covetousness*, wickedness, deceit, lasciviousness, an evil eye, blasphemy, pride, foolishness: all these evil things come from within, and defile the man" (Mark 7: 21-23). Covetousness is here ranked with a list of

149

"things" that Christ calls "evil," and they are said to have a degrading and degenerating effect upon men.

The word "covet" means to have an inordinate desire to possess. We covet when we set our hearts upon something, especially that which belongs to another. Often desire has so obsessed a man's heart that he has stooped to gain it by unlawful means. Our Lord warned: "Take heed, and beware of covetousness" (Luke 12: 15). It is doubtless a characteristic of the wicked and unregenerate, for the covetous man is classed with those who are "filled with all unrighteousness, fornication, wickedness" (Rom. 1: 29). The Apostle adds elsewhere that the covetous man is no better than the whoremonger, nor unclean person, and that he has no inheritance in the kingdom of Christ and of God (Eph. 5: 5).

The command was given in order that men might be forewarned against this deadly evil. Paul said: "I had not known sin but by the Law, for I had not known lust, except the Law had said, Thou shalt not covet" (Rom. 7: 7, 8). That which God forbids in the Tenth Commandment is enlarged upon and illuminated by Saint Paul's text. To covet is to lust, and it is so heinous a sin that the Bible places it among the grosser crimes that will shut out a man from Heaven.

We covet when we allow our wants to rule over us. God has promised in His Word that He will supply *all* our need, but nowhere is it stated that we shall have all that we want. Our wants should be subject to His perfect will as it is revealed in His Word.

On one occasion our Lord said: "Beware of covetousness: for a man's life consisteth not in the abundance of the things which he possesseth" (Luke 12: 15). This warning was prompted by the presence in the audience of a covetous man who interrupted Jesus by saying: "Master, speak to my brother, that he divide the inheritance with me." This man was covetous. If he had not been, our Lord would not have said what He did. The man was taken up more with earthly possessions than he was with Christ's message of eternal life. He made the mistake of grasping selfishly after earthly things, and these can never give us peace and joy. The covetous man is so taken up with the affairs of this life that he seldom thinks of preparing for eternity. Beware of covetousness!

Covetousness is a sin of the heart, often leading to outward acts of sin. In a very real sense it is the root of many other forms of evil. In the case of Achan covetousness led to theft. Complete victory of Israel over Jericho rested upon the condition that no Israelite keep any part of the spoils. All was to be brought into the treasury of the Lord (Josh. 6: 18, 19). The morning after the fall of Jericho every Israelite awoke with a clear conscience except Achan. He stole from the spoils "a goodly Babylonish garment, and two hundred shekels of silver, and a wedge of gold of fifty shekels weight" (Josh. 7: 21). When Joshua discovered the sin, Achan confessed: "I *coveted* them, and took them." If Achan had mastered the sinful desire when it struck first at his heart, he never would have yielded to the temptation to steal.

There is a clear case of evil concupiscence charged against Ahab when he coveted Naboth's vineyard. Ahab's passion to possess stirred up Jezebel, so that she employed the sons of Belial to bear false witness against Naboth, and finally to cause his death (1 Kings

21: 1-16). God did not allow Ahab to go unpunished
for his sin. The wicked king was slain, and the dogs
came and licked his blood in the very place where
dogs licked the blood of Naboth. Let us beware of
covetousness!

The peril of covetousness is no more obvious than
in the sin of David. God had said: "Thou shalt not
covet thy neighbor's wife." When the evil desire arose
in David's heart to have Bath-sheba the wife of Uriah,
the lustful passion in David's heart got the better of
him. He yielded to his desires, and in addition to
violating the Tenth Commandment he violated the
Seventh also. The Apostle Paul warns believers of
the possibility of falling into David's sin, when he said:
"But fornication, and all uncleanness, or covetousness,
let it not be once named among you, as becometh
saints" (Eph. 5: 3). Beware of covetousness!

It was covetousness that lead Ananias and Sapphira
to lie about their goods. When they sold their possessions, they kept back part of the price, pretending
all the while that they had given all. Peter charged
Ananias with telling a lie, and God struck both him
and his wife dead. Beware of covetousness!

Covetousness makes a man mean and selfish. The
covetous spirit in Lot tempted him to take advantage
of his more generous uncle. He chose the best for himself and left Abraham to take what remained. If Lot
has mastered his desires he would have manifested a
more generous spirit toward Abraham.

Judas is an example as to how far the sin of covetousness will drive its victim. "What will ye give me?"
asked Judas, "and I will deliver Him unto you" (Matt.
26: 15). Judas' love of money lured him into the

betrayal of his most trusted Friend. When the sin of covetousness had finished with Judas, it sent him to a suicide's grave without wealth in his hands and without Christ in his heart. As far as we know, Judas was of little, if any, practical good on earth. It is a common saying, that a hog is good for nothing while he is alive. You cannot ride him like the horse; you cannot use him to draw like the ox; he does not provide clothing like the sheep; nor milk like the cow; he will not guard the house like the dog. He is good only for the slaughter. Like the hog, a covetous man is of little worth while he lives, for he does no good with his possessions. When he is dead, his goods are disposed of, and he uses them no more for his wallowing in the mire of sin.

When a man becomes drugged with the spirit of covetousness it may lead him to depart from the faith. The Scriptures declare: "They that will be rich fall into temptation and a snare, and into many foolish and hurtful lusts, which drown men in destruction and perdition. For the love of money is the root of all evil: which while some coveted after, they have erred from the faith, and pierced themselves through with many sorrows" (1 Tim. 6: 9, 10). Christians therefore need to be warned lest we set our hearts and our affections on the things of this earth. "Alas, there are church-members who, fascinated by this seemingly fair and innocent flower, have forsaken the pilgrim's path to pluck it: but it was only to find themselves wounded by its many thorns." Do not boast of your immunity from the temptation to covet. Its roots are deep in the fallen nature of every true believer so that we must say with the Apostle: "The good that I would I do not:

but the evil which I would not, that I do . . . I find then a law, that, when I would do good, evil is present with me" (Rom. 7: 19, 21). Beloved Christian, let us heed our Lord's tender pleading and beware of covetousness.

We know "that in the last days perilous times shall come. For men shall be lovers of their own selves, *covetous*" (2 Tim. 3: 1, 2). Though covetousness shall abound in the last days we may be sure that it is an abomination to the Lord. "For the wicked boasteth of his heart's desire, and blesseth the covetous, whom the Lord abhorreth" (Ps. 10: 3). If we turn from this sin we shall be rewarded even in this life, for, "He that hateth covetousness shall prolong his days" (Prov. 28: 16).

2. THE CURE.

The Bible not only speaks out in condemnation against covetousness but offers the best cure for all who have been poisoned by it. Before we consider the remedy for a covetous spirit, let it be said that it is lawful and possible for a man to desire to make good in business and to increase his holdings without having a covetous heart. Furthermore, it is clear that God would expect us to be diligent and conservative for the welfare of our families. Believers are exhorted not to be "slothful in business" (Rom. 12: 11). To work honestly toward the acquisition of a private estate is provided for in God's Word. What is forbidden is the setting of the heart on securing wealth through covetousness.

Unlawful covetousness may be cured by lawful covetousness as taught by the Apostle Paul. For example, we are encouraged to, "Covet earnestly the best gifts" (1 Cor. 12: 31). It is right for a Christian to desire to cultivate his talents and to improve his usefulness for the Lord provided he is not motivated by any selfish interest. It is natural for the heart and the mind to be active in meditation and thought. Only let us be certain that we can say with David: "Let the . . . meditation of my heart be acceptable in Thy sight, O Lord" (Ps. 19: 14). "Finally, brethren, whatsoever things are true . . . whatsoever things are pure, whatsoever things are lovely, whatsoever things are of good report . . . think on these things" (Phil. 4: 8). This is lawful covetousness, and when it is practised daily in our lives we will have little time or be able to give little thought to grasping after things greedily for our own personal gain.

Covetousness may be cured also by contentment. Sometimes we become dissatisfied and discontented with God's provision for us. When looking upon the prosperity or the wealth of others as compared with the little we have, we feel that we have been slighted. Do not forget that our Father has promised to supply all our need. Paul said: "My God shall supply all your need according to His riches in glory by Christ Jesus" (Phil. 4: 19). Certainly it would not be good for all men to be wealthy. It has been said that, "In our possessions, as with our garments, not that which is largest, but that which fits us best, is best for us." Let the godly learn this truth and they shall increase in heavenly riches for, "A little that a righteous man hath is better than the riches of many wicked" (Ps. 37: 16).

Most of us need to learn the lesson that God taught to the Apostle Paul. He testifies: "I have learned, in whatsoever state I am, to be content" (Phil. 4: 11). Here was something that Paul had not always known. Reared in luxury, he never knew what it meant to be in want. But circumstances had taught Paul that his sufficiency was in Christ. He learned to be content because he was dependent upon Christ.

The unholy, complaining, discontented spirit that is seen in so many professing Christians does not have the approval of God. It is displeasing to the Almighty. I once read a story of a Quaker who was so convinced that no one was fully satisfied with his lot in life, that he erected a sign near the highway on his ten-acre tract of land, which read: "This ten-acre tract will be given to the one who is perfectly content. Apply . . . . ." The writer of the story went on to state that it was not long before a man knocked at his door. The Quaker opened it, and inquired, "What can I do for thee, friend?"

His visitor replied, "As I was driving down the road, I noticed your sign that says you will give this ten-acre piece of land to the one who is perfectly content. Do you really mean that?"

"Yes, friend, I mean exactly that."

"Then, mister, you don't have to wait any longer. I'm here to claim it."

"But may I first inquire of thee," said the Quaker, "if thou dost feel that thou hast a right to make such a claim? Art thou perfectly content with thy lot in life? Art thou satisfied with such things as thou hast?"

"Yes, certainly," came the quick reply. "I'm happy and satisfied. Life has been good to me. I have nothing to complain about. I'm perfectly content."

"Then, my friend," continued the Quaker, "if thou art perfectly content with life as thou hast found it, and with such possessions as thou hast, why shouldst thou desire these ten acres?"

Many of us are like the disillusioned man who was sure that he was satisfied with his lot in life until he discovered that more was available. Then it was that he became discontented and covetous. Would you be rich, dear friend? Listen to what the Bible has to say—

"But godliness with contentment is great gain"
(1 Tim. 6: 6).

Then, too, confidence in God is a sure cure for covetousness. Ofttimes we covet when we become overanxious. Anxiety leads to worry, and worry is a sin. When we worry we are not trusting our heavenly Father. Cares lead to covetousness. We need to learn to trust in the Lord. "Cast thy burden upon the Lord, and He shall sustain thee: He shall never suffer the righteous to be moved" (Ps. 55: 22). "Commit thy way unto the Lord; trust also in Him; and He shall bring it to pass" (Ps. 37: 5). The Apostle Peter said: "Casting all your care upon Him; for He careth for you" (1 Pet. 5: 7). Paul adds: "Be careful for nothing; but in everything by prayer and supplication with thanksgiving let your requests be made known unto God" (Phil. 4: 6). The Christians at Philippi were constantly worrying, and Paul was exhorting them to stop it. He wanted them worrying about "nothing," which means literally, "not even one thing." A cure for covetousness is to stop worrying, and a cure for worry is believing prayer.

God is a great Provider. He cares for all of His creation. He cares for you. If you trust Him fully there will be no occasion for worry or anxiety, and you will not be apt to be overcome by covetousness. Why do you not trust Him? To covet what another man possesses is folly. Only God can provide.

Finally, covetousness gives evidence that we do not love God as we ought. We conquer covetousness when we do not allow our love for the Lord to grow cold. The dainties of this world are spread attractively before us, and they bid for our affections. When we fix our gaze upon those forbidden values that we know we are not to have, then it is that we weaken, become fretful, and covetous. But as we refuse to allow our love for Christ to grow cold, we can say "no" to the things of the world. God desires our perfect and undivided love towards Him, and when we respond whole-heartedly He enables us to turn from the beggarly elements of this world. We are exhorted: "Set your affection on things above, not on things on the earth" (Col. 3: 2). Jesus asks: "Lovest thou Me more than these"? We should be able to answer "Yea, Lord; Thou knowest that I love *Thee*" (John 21: 15).

There is no sin so deadly and damaging as covetousness. Here lies the root cause of the violation of every other commandment in the Decalogue. Dr. Morgan has said: "Out of disobedience to this command will spring sins that break every law written upon the second Table of the Law. It is the sin of covetousness that makes it possible for a man to say, 'It is Corban,' of possessions he should use in honoring his father and his mother. Criminal records will prove that, in a great majority of cases, unholy desire was the inspiration of murder. No word need be written to demonstrate the fact that the look of concupiscence ever precedes the act of adultery. Theft of every description is the offspring of desire to possess that which is unreachable by lawful means. The evil spirit that makes false witness possible is motivated far more often than perhaps appears by covetous aspiration. Thus the whole realm of human inter-relation is disorganized and broken up by the dishonoring of the tenth commandment."

Let us pray with the Psalmist: "Incline my heart unto Thy testimonies, and not to covetousness" (Ps. 119: 36).

CHAPTER XII
THE SOVEREIGN LAW OF LOVE

THE ELEVENTH COMMANDMENT

"A new commandment I give unto you, That ye love one another; as I have loved you, that ye also love one another" (John 13: 34).

THE SOVEREIGN LAW OF LOVE

"A new commandment I give unto you, That ye love one another; as I have loved you, that ye also love one another" (John 13: 34).

A MAN who is about to leave this life will doubtless express the deepest feelings of his soul. One may not realize that death is near, and die in silence. But when our Lord knew that His hour had come, He gathered His disciples about Him and spoke to them concerning the deep things of God. There were statements uttered by Christ in the Passover Chamber that the disciples had never heard before. It was in the Upper Room of fellowship where He spoke about "The love of Christ which passeth knowledge" (Eph. 3: 19). In issuing this New Commandment, "That ye love one another," He was setting forth the Sovereign Law of Christian Love. Whatever authority of divine approval accompanied the Mosaic Law, we may be sure that this Sovereign Law carries the same authority *plus* the Personal testimony of the living Christ.

1. THE PATTERN OF CHRISTIAN LOVE.

The New Commandment that the Lord Jesus enjoined upon His friends and followers He had faithfully demonstrated before them by His life. And now it is to cost Him that life to utter the words: "As I have loved you." Indeed, Christ alone was the perfect Pattern of Love. He alone could interpret the word in its fullest meaning. If we are to learn the Law of Love we must look at God's Son, for in Him is the love of God perfected. "God commendeth His love toward us, in that, while we were yet sinners, *Christ died for us*" (Rom. 5: 8).

In ages past God had been speaking through His prophets at different times and in various ways, revealing Himself as the God of holiness, might, truth, and mercy. But not until Jesus Christ came into the world had man known fully the love of God. In more ways than one the angels are superior to men, and for centuries they too were God's messengers to reveal Himself to the world. But when prophets or angels stand beside the Son of God it is evident that He holds the position of incomparable majesty and glory. God "hath in these last days spoken unto us by His Son" (Heb. 1: 2). The heart of the Father was never fully revealed in His infinite love until His only begotten Son left Heaven to dwell among men. Jesus is the highest revelation of God. God is love, and, "No man hath seen God at any time; the only begotten Son, which is in the bosom of the Father, He hath declared (or fully revealed) Him" (John 1: 18).

We can see in Christ the Pattern of Love in His submission. Only love could draw the Eternal One from the Ivory Palaces into a world of woe. The riches of Heaven and earth were His. "Though He was rich, yet for your sakes He became poor, that ye through His poverty might be rich" (2 Cor. 8: 9). What condescending love! He was born in a borrowed manger, traveled in a borrowed boat, rode on a borrowed beast, worshipped in a borrowed room, and was buried in a borrowed tomb. Such submission could be prompted only by self-sacrificing love. It was a love equal to and identical with the love of the Father. "Even as the Father hath loved Me, I also have loved you, abide ye in My love."

Christ is the Pattern of Divine Love in the deeds that He performed. His whole life was a constant ministry of sacrificial love. He went about doing good. He moved among men with the single purpose of helping them. The sick and the sorrowing welcomed the healing ministry of the Great Physician. In love and compassion the Perfect Man went to where men were and did for them what no other could do. Love led Him to social outcasts and physical derelicts. The Son of Man ministered to the poorest and lowest of men. During the closing moments of His earthly life as He hung suspended between Heaven and earth on Calvary's Cross, divine love was expressed in His prayer for His enemies when He cried: "Father, forgive them; for they know not what they do" (Luke 23: 34).

The magnitude and might of perfect love was nowhere exemplified as it was in Christ's Death for sinners. His life and deeds wonderfully revealed Divine love, but we are right when we declare that the sacrificial death of our Lord Jesus Chrsit is the highest expression of redeeming love. The Saviour Himself said: "Greater love hath no man than this, that a man lay down his life for his friends" (John 15: 13). The Apostle John adds: "Hereby perceive we the love of God, because He laid down His life for us" (1 John 3: 16). Nothing but love would allow a holy and sovereign God to stoop to wash away the sins of such unworthy subjects as we are. So we sing with the apostle of love: "Unto Him who loved us, and washed us from our sins in His own blood" (Rev. 1: 5). Only as we reach a true estimate of what it cost our God and His Christ to redeem us from sin and death can we testify with Paul of "The Son of God, who loved me, and gave Himself for me" (Gal. 2: 20). In the midst of His life and labors Christ loved us with an undying love, and then, "Having loved His own which were in the world, He loved them unto the end" (John 13: 1). Praise God! This love is ours to experience and enjoy now.

But the display of divine love did not terminate at the cross. Calvary was not the consummation of the Saviour's compassion. He arose and ascended on high in continued expressions of His love. If we go back to the passage in Rev. 1: 5, we note that the Revised Version reads: "Unto Him that *loveth* us." Here it is in the present tense, and it expresses the perpetuity and protraction of the love of the Risen Christ. The Epistle to the Hebrews reflects the same truth when it states: "He ever *liveth* to make intercession for them" (Heb. 7: 25). And again: "Christ is . . . entered . . . into heaven itself, *now* to appear in the presence of God for us" (Heb. 9: 24). Thus we see the sovereign law of love continuing to operate in the intercessory work of the Ascended Lord.

2. THE POWER OF CHRISTIAN LOVE.

Love is one of the grandest themes in all the Holy Scriptures. More wonderful still is its far-reaching effect upon the human race. Only eternity will reveal the countless number of lives that have been won and mastered by love.   Pagan powers and satanic systems have been smitten wherever the Love of Christ has been preached and lived.   When every other effort has failed, love will break through and triumph.

Before we look at the power of love in operation, it might be well to state that the Law of Love is not a new one.   One day a lawyer, seeking to entangle our Lord in His speech, asked Him: "Master, which is the great commandment in the law?   Jesus said unto him, Thou shalt love the Lord thy God with all thy heart, and with all thy soul, and with all thy mind.   This is the first and great commandment.   And the second is like unto it, Thou shalt love thy neighbor as thyself."

"On these two commandments hang all the law and the prophets" (Matt. 22: 35-40).

The hundreds of commandments embodied by the Mosaic Code are here summarized by Christ when He declared that, basically, that code is love.   It was an Old Testament quotation found in Deut. 6: 4, 5 and in Lev. 19: 18.   This new commandment, therefore, expresses what was intended in the Old; namely, that love is the fulfilment of the Law.

We have seen something of divine love expressed in Christ the Perfect Pattern, and the influence that it exercised.   Let us look now at the influence of that same love when it is given a chance to operate in the life of a Christian.   There is never an expression of divine love where one has not been made a partaker of the divine nature.   Contrariwise, it is possible for every regenerate child of God to show forth this love, "because the love of God is shed abroad in our hearts by the Holy Ghost which is given unto us" (Rom. 5: 5). It is as the indwelling Spirit controls us completely that we are able to demonstrate His love to others.

Obedience to the law of love will wield mighty power with God and man. Nothing impressed the pagans of the genuineness of the early Church as much as the demonstration of divine love in the lives of the believers. The love that drew the heathen to Christ is not human love alone, nor is it divine love alone, but rather is it the combination of both in the lives of those of us who are Christ's followers.

The pre-eminence and the power of love is beautifully expressed in the first eulogy of Christian love the world has ever known. The influence of love is thus portrayed by the Apostle in First Corinthians. In a splendid exposition of verses four to seven, Dr. Scroggie gives the following analysis—

1. Love is not Hasty, but Patient.
   It "suffereth long" (ver. 4).

2. Love is not Inconsiderate, but Benevolent.
   It "is kind" (ver. 4).

3. Love is not Envious, but Content.
   It "envieth not" (ver. 4).

4. Love is not Boastful, but Unostentatious.
   It "vaunteth not itself" (ver. 4).

5. Love is not Arrogant, but Humble.
   It "is not puffed up" (ver. 4).

6. Love is not Rude, but Courteous.
   It "doth not behave itself unseemly" (ver. 5).

7. Love is not Selfish, but Self-forgetful.
   It "seeketh not her own" (ver. 5).

8. Love is not Irritable, but Good-tempered.
   "Is not easily provoked" (ver. 5).

9. Love is not Vindictive, but Generous.
   It "thinketh no evil" (ver. 5).

10. Love is not Malevolent, but High-principled.
    "Rejoiceth not in iniquity, but rejoiceth in
        the truth" (ver. 6).

11. Love is not Rebellious, but Brave.
    It "beareth all things" (ver. 7).

12. Love is not Suspicious, but Confident.
    It "believeth all things" (ver. 7).

13. Love is not Despondent, but Undiscourageable.
    It "hopeth all things" (ver. 7).

14. Love is not Conquerable, but Indomitable.
    It "endureth all things" (ver. 7).

And then Paul reaches the peak of this conception of love by stating, "Love never faileth." Love lasts because in it there are no elements of deterioration. Love remains strong and steadfast. All about us we see change and decay, but love moves strongly and steadily onward, animating and accelerating each life that yields to its Author. In the darkest night love shines through by keeping its face to the dawn. In the fiercest battle love withstands when the onslaught of the enemy is strongest. When despised and rejected love does not become bitter and resentful within. Love is the divine dynamic for successful living. S. D. Gordon has said:

"Peace is love resting: Prayer is love keeping tryst: Conflict with sin is love jealously fighting for its lover: Hatred of sin is love shrinking from that which separates from its lover: Sympathy is love feeling: Enthusiasm is love burning: Hope is love expecting: Patience is love waiting: Modesty is love keeping out of sight: Soul-winning is love pleading: Bible study is love reading the letters of its Beloved."

There is no higher accomplishment in one's life than to love as Christ loved. The Apostle Paul became the greatest and most useful instrument in God's hands because he was constrained by the love of Christ (2 Cor. 5: 14). His aspirations are the highest who is motivated by divine love. The most humble of God's children who can do the least for Him, if transformed by love become of more value than the loveless soul, even though the latter be most gifted and talented. A man may strive to keep the law, but when love is absent he strives in vain, for, "Love is the fulfilling of the law" (Rom. 13: 10).

3. THE PROGRAM OF CHRISTIAN LOVE.

The question arises in some minds as to how far one must go in keeping this First and Greatest Commandment. We cannot settle this question by human reasoning. There are those who are unlovely and unloveable from whom we would turn in a moment. To exercise and express love to these would be to us like casting pearls before swine. And yet, if we are to comply with our Lord's program, "As I have loved you," we must remember that His love found expression toward thieves, harlots, and those who were His worst enemies. If we desire to become obedient to His command we must follow the divine order.

First, we must love God. To some this may seem like a superfluous demand. Perhaps you are as others who cast the resentful reply that they do not hate God. But exactly what is the extent of your love toward your Lord? We must keep before us the majestic truth that the very essence of His Being is love. "God is love" (1 John 4: 8). Because of what God is, He loves us with an everlasting love, and enables us to love Him. The deepest devotion to our heavenly Father will be love without a limit. Such love shows itself in unlimited sacrifice. Even as Christ loved us and gave Himself for us; so ought we to love Him and give ourselves to Him. Love is not magnified alone in actions. A helpless cripple may give evidence of the deepest devotion toward God. To love our Lord with the heart, soul, and might gives expression of the largeness of the soul. Let us learn the new commandment of the Son of God, and love Him even as He loves us. An appreciation of His love toward us is the basis of our love to Him, for "to whom little is forgiven, the same loveth little" (Luke 7: 47).

We are to love the Holy Scriptures. Jesus warned His disciples against being "ashamed of Me and of My words" (Luke 9: 26). We boast of having faith in the Bible while we sit in ignorance of its contents. We speak out against the false teachers, but we are unable to give an intelligent refutation of their pernicious doctrine. We testify to the saving power of the Word, but refuse to take it to those who are dying in their sins. We will not speak out against it, but neither do we allow it to speak to us. There is a sad neglect of the personal study of God's Holy Word, and all because we do not love it as we ought. The Psalmist testifies: "How sweet are Thy words unto my taste! Yea, sweeter than honey to my mouth" (Ps. 119: 103). As we ponder God's Treasury of Truth for our personal profit we come to love it more. There is needed today a revival of Bible study in the homes of Christians. We give more time to the reading of novels and magazines than we do to the Holy Bible. We prove our love for the Word of God as we delve deeply into its mighty truth, practise its precepts, and distribute it to others. When we starve our souls our faith will wane, for "Faith cometh by hearing, and hearing by the Word of God" (Rom. 10: 17).

"Great peace have they which love Thy law"
(Ps. 119: 165).

Besides, we are to love our neighbors. After our Lord had stated the first and greatest commandment, He added: "And the second is like, namely this, Thou shalt love thy neighbor as thyself. There is none other commandment greater than these" (Mark 12: 30, 31). Our love to God and to His Word will express itself in our daily living. Our relationship to our fellow-men in everyday-life is the outgrowth of our relation to God. The Apostle John says: "But whoso hath this world's good, and seeth his brother have need, and shutteth up his bowels of compassion from him, *how dwelleth the love of God in him?*" (1 John 3: 17). Our love to man, God's creature, is never to be compared with our love to God Himself. God is to receive our deepest devotion and highest affection. He must always have the pre-eminence. Christ's teaching on this subject is not to be misunderstood. No amount of neighborliness or humanitarianism can save the soul of him who performs good deeds. When Jesus taught the scribe on this subject His last words to His questioner were: "Thou art not far from the kingdom of God" (Mark 12: 34). He was not far from it, but yet he was not in it. This commandment was not given in order that it might save. It reveals the true spirit of those who already are saved. The command is a challenge especially when our neighbor has sought to make himself our enemy. Nevertheless our Lord says: "Love your enemies, do good to them which hate you" (Luke 6: 27). Let us exercise the greatest of care so that we do not become bitter because of the world's hatred for us. Just as soon as we become morose over the treatment of our enemies against us, then it is that we lose our testimony. Love knows no bounds nor limitations, but it reaches out to the uttermost, rendering to all a sincere and energetic devotion.

Finally, we are to love the brethren. This is the needed note in the Church of Christ today. There is a blighting inconsistency when we preach the love of God and hate our brother in Christ. Such preaching bears no fruit. We merely become stones of stumbling to those to whom we have ministered. The gospel that we preach is the message of life and love, but the life of the minister must conform to his message. "He that hateth his brother is in darkness, and walketh in darkness, and knoweth not whither he goeth, because that darkness hath blinded his eyes" (1 John 2: 11). Jesus said: "If ye keep My commandments, ye shall abide in My love" (John 15: 10). And what are His commandments? They are two, and together they form the highest calling and commandment ever issued to man—

"And this is His commandment, That we should believe on the Name of His Son Jesus Christ, AND LOVE ONE ANOTHER, as He gave us commandment"

(1 John 3: 23).

Believing on Jesus Christ makes us Christians. Loving one another makes us obedient Christians. It has been said that as the spokes of a wheel approach their center, they approach each other. So also, when men are brought to Jesus Christ, the center of life and joy and hope and love, they are drawn toward each other in Christian love. And the closer they are to Christ the Center, the closer they are to each other in love.

Beloved, let us love one another, for love is the fulfilling of the law.

BIBLIOGRAPHY

"UNIVERSITY LECTURES ON THE TEN COMMANDMENTS,"
   by George Dana Boardman.

"TEN RULES FOR LIVING,"
   by Clovis G. Chappell.

"THE TEN COMMANDMENTS,"
   by William Dallman.

"THE LAW OF THE SABBATH AND THE NEW WORLD ORDER,"
   by M. R. DeHaan.

"SERMONS ON THE TEN COMMANDMENTS,"
   by William Masselink.

"THE TEN COMMANDMENTS,"
   by G. Campbell Morgan.

"THE END OF THE SABBATH,"
   by Harry Rimmer.

"OUGHT CHRISTIANS TO KEEP THE SABBATH?"
   by R. A. Torrey.

INDEX OF SCRIPTURE TEXTS

177